Den of Thieves

Misappropriation of Divine Stewardship in the Church

To: Bella

A Great woman

From: Rev. William Neill

with Thanks

Den of Thieves

MISAPPROPRIATION OF DIVINE STEWARDSHIP IN THE CHURCH

Based on the Scriptural Text of Jesus in Matthew

WILLIAM L. NEILL

Den of Thieves
Misappropriation of Divine Stewardship in the Church

Published by Wheatmark®
610 East Delano Street, Suite 104
Tucson, Arizona 85705 U.S.A.
www.wheatmark.com

International Standard Book Number: 978-1-60494-080-0
Library of Congress Control Number: 2008921004

CONTENTS

Part IV: The Propositions

PREFACE

And said unto them, It is written, My house shall be called the house of prayer; but ye have made it a den of thieves. (Matt. 21:13)

This famous verse shows Jesus furious at the Jerusalem Temple authorities. These leaders had betrayed the faithful and needy by enriching themselves at the expense of the poor, by luxuriating in their own power while ignoring God's call to love one another and exemplify that by meeting the needs of the people.

In our own time, church leaders are similarly betraying those who come to worship, who count on the church to care about them and heal their woes. Just as Jesus was angry about these wrongdoings by those entrusted with stewardship of the faith community, those of us who see similar wrongs in these times should also be angry. Jesus showed us that we must challenge the leadership, both laypersons and clergy, when they steal from the mouths of the poor and exploit relationships. We must call our faith leaders to accountability.

I wrote this book out of the same anger and concern—anger and concern that has built over the past twenty-two years of pastoral experience. It is an anger rooted in frustration and intimidation. It is an anger that burns with hurt and disappointment about the misapplication of Jesus' model of church and Christian stewardship.

My hope and purpose is to provoke the leadership of the church to move with integrity toward biblical principles of proper fiscal and relationship stewardship as we build organisms and organizations to advance the kingdom of God.

My secondary purpose is to battle a great sickness in the church. Congregations must do battle against the many spiritual hindrances self-inflicted by their own lack of awareness and perpetrated upon them by improper leadership.

Many people know and can attest to the widespread practices of misappropriation, misapplication, and mismanagement; borderline fraud, embezzlement, and undue influence purely for personal financial gain and power that take place in the church on a week-to-week basis. These practices have often been accepted as commonplace, to the extent that much spiritual damage has been done to individuals, congregations, and the body of Christ as a whole. A trend has taken place that will fuel a fire of self-destruction if careful intervention does not occur to dampen the flames. We can see the sickness in the church when those who cry "Fire" are accused by those involved and called deranged, jealous, envious, and nonconforming. After denouncing the one who would shine light on the problem, the happy perpetrator exclaims, "All is well."

Here is the dilemma of a pastor or layperson who sees the games being played. You know about the unethical practices, the sickness. You, people who know they should speak out but won't, feel deterred from exposing the disease because of job security, misplaced or blind loyalty, favors, and of course payoffs or hush funds. And then you have this ball in the pit of your stomach that won't let you rest until you see an end to this tragedy, coupled with an undying commitment to a just and merciful God.

Now you see why I write this book.

It was clear to me that one of the consequences of writing a book like this might be ridicule, but with prayer, discussion, and careful thought, I proceeded, because I was certain that I was led by God! It is my sincere desire that the messages of this book will be received with the same concern that I brought to the writing of it. My hope is that the church accepts the diagnosis that we are sick when it comes to our stewardship and that we then do what it takes to become healed, so we can join Jesus in the call to live into the radical and holy vision of jubilee:

> The Spirit of the Lord is upon me, because he hath anointed me to preach the gospel to the poor; he hath sent me to heal the broken-hearted, to preach deliverance to the captives, and recovering of sight to the blind, to set at liberty them that are bruised, to preach the acceptable year of the Lord. (Luke 4:18-19)

Part One will aid the reader to access the first step in any healing process: a diagnosis, examination, and analysis of the symptoms.

Part Two takes the healing process a step further by enabling the reader to give a proper prognosis of the underlying causes—to acknowledge the sickness.

Part Three will offer a practical prescription that will attack the bacterial pollutants within the body of Christ. As with any prescription, it is effective only when the directions are followed, regardless of the size of the body or duration of the sickness. The prescription is guaranteed to heal, producing a healthy body that will be engulfed with the necessary nutrients for prevention of further sickness.

Part Four establishes propositions of a consistent return to the prescribed intake of a daily dosage of right stewardship practices, enabling the body to fight further infection of robbers and thieves.

Note: References to Scripture in English come from the traditional King James Version of the Bible, and definitions of Greek and Hebrew references come from *Strong's Exhaustive Concordance*, *Young's Analytical Concordance to the Bible*, the *Wycliffe Dictionary of Theology*, and *Vine's Expository Dictionary of Old and New Testament Words*. Other definitions come from the Thorndike and Barnhart *World Book Dictionary*.

ACKNOWLEDGMENTS

It is incumbent upon me to acknowledge the one true friend I can count on at any time. His constant inspiration has, for all of my life, been the source of consistent being. He has listened to my complaints, my self-pity, my anger, bitterness, and gossip, all without fear of hearing it again. He has extended to me the kind of patience that only a father could bestow. His guidance has provided the order of my footsteps. His counsel continues to discipline the thoughts of my heart. His wisdom transforms my limited knowledge to a practical understanding of life's journey. To speak of his steadfast love is to bathe in the calm assurance and peaceful bliss of a daddy's promise, provision, and protection. I speak of and acknowledge God Almighty, the is that was and is to come. To his Son, my beloved Savior and Redeemer, in whom I live, move, and have my being, Jesus, the one called Christ, I am eternally grateful for the debt paid—I owe. All praises to the third person of the Triune God, but in no wise the least, the Holy Spirit, who gives a constant and steady drumbeat of sustentation to this wonderful experience called living! I praise and glorify you to the highest for all the many unmerited blessings you have bestowed upon me.

The Bible is explicit in its suggestion that a man should have his own wife (1 Cor. 7:2). "Whoso findeth a wife findeth a good thing, and obtaineth favor of the Lord" (Prov. 18:22); and "marriage is honorable in all, and the bed undefiled" (Heb. 13:4a). I can truly say that the Lord has provided me with that helpmeet, suitable for the Adamic nature I carry. She is one who submits to and subscribes to the very essence of a virtuous woman. To speak of her loyalty, while I am being molded to what God would have me become, is to cherish her vow made to me thirty-two years ago. To my darling wife, Shirley, your presence in my life has given me the balance necessary to make a man complete. Thank you for all your love, your gentleness, your kind existence, and your pleasant demeanor. I love you more than this life will afford me time to demonstrate!

The Bible is once again exact in its narrative of what children are to a father. Although I did not experience the real essence of fatherhood with my firstborn, Carlos Maurice Shipman, I can truly say I am proud of his home training and how that true instruction has molded him into a fine young man, now a pastor following the prerogative of God. Trust me when I say that I love you and regret only that I did not have the wonderful experience of having you in my household during your years growing up. To say that I was a deadbeat dad who did not want that experience is nothing more than a lie of the devil. I'm proud to be your dad.

To Mario and Sabrina, my twins, you have been a handful over the years. When I think about your births, how I could hold you, one in each hand, and to see you as graduates of high school and now college, I get choked up inside. You are the epitome of God's grace! When I see so many twins born with debilitating deformities, I thank God for his mercy toward you. You are great children. I am so proud of you. You have given my life reins of direction and boundaries. I am looking forward to being around when you too can experience this joy.

I also acknowledge with joy two wonderful grandsons: C. J. and Tyshon. They give me the wonderful experience of seeing what was in their father when he was their age. I love you much.

My life has been filled with so many wonderful people. This book cannot afford me enough pages to mention them all. Each person I have had the opportunity to share with has given me something to cherish the rest of my life. The churches I have pastored have given me the kind of instruction and life experience that no institution of higher learning could do.

The business I was a part of more than twenty years ago, the former A. L. Williams sales and marketing organization, as well as the wonderful people who shared that experience with me, has proven to be the most rewarding secular career experience of all in my life. Here's why. In this business success was based on helping others to achieve rather than success at the expense of others. What a tremendous journey into the world of comrades with a cause! I found that this business experience was right for me and taught me many valuable lessons that I took to the world of the church.

To my many colleagues in ministry, fellow yokefellows of the sacred gospel of our Lord Jesus Christ, thanks are due to him for the tremendous opportunity of laboring with you. I am blessed by your dedication to ministry; your unwavering faith in God; your frustrations, internal wrestling, and strife with rigid structures that have allowed some to feel they have no voice. Your obedience to your calls in the midst of weariness and constant resistance is truly one of my greatest inspirations for producing this work. May the God by whom you are called favor you with a bounteous blessing.

To a wonderful friend who inspired me to keep my radical nature, Barbara Zelter, thanks for not changing and for the much-needed editorial advice.

Finally, I want to acknowledge my father, William D. Neill, Jr., of Bladen County, North Carolina, who has been a tremendous source of inspiration, guidance, and strength. Daddy, I am so proud to be your son and glad you are my daddy. I thank you for the rod of correction, the firmness by which you molded me. The home you constructed for the kind of nurture that you and Mom provided for seven children is the one I have tried to imitate for my family.

To my remaining three brothers, Darryl, Jerrod, and Craig, and my one sister, Shermetta, your love and prayers will never be forgotten or forsaken. I am happy to acknowledge the inspiration I have received from each of you over the years of our growing up. I would not want any other brothers and sister to be my siblings. I love you all and give thanks.

I am blessed to have a good cadre of nieces and nephews who I am compelled to be an example for in producing this work. I pray for you each day.

I must also acknowledge other relatives who have shown me the value of family and kinship. I want to say to you what so many wait to say at funerals: you are so dear to my heart.

To my mother-in-law, Mary A. McCall, and my sisters-in-law, Agnes and Bertha, I give thanks for our loving and strong relationships over the years. To my other sisters-in law, Lois and Bertie, you mean so much to me.

It is with a sense of bittersweet sorrow that I acknowledge my dear sweet mother, Eunice; two brothers, Harry and Michael; two grandfathers, William D. Neill Sr. and West Young; and two grandmothers, Lena Neill and Evelina Young; who now taste unmingled love beyond degree. I dedicate this work to their memories for the love they had for the church and her husband, Jesus, a love that they not only talked about but lived through their service and sacrifice. I have never nor will I ever forget you. I love you still!

Sincerely,
William L. Neill

INTRODUCTION

When we consider the nature of the institution called the church, a number of opinions come to mind from a variety of people who make up that institution. After twenty-two years of pastoral ministry, it is obvious to me that many really do not understand the nature of the church nor the practical principles that ensure the success of this sacred entity. For years the church has been made up of individuals who show up each week, rush to get there, rush to get out, and then go back to business as usual for the remainder of the week. They view the church as a weekend hustle or something that is merely a habit for those who have nothing else to do.

The church is both an organization and an organism. It is an organization because we must handle the business affairs of congregations and larger denominational units. That is, staff must be hired, budgets must be made and honored, buildings must be built, and ministries must be managed in ways that are legal and accountable. It is an organism, a living entity, because it is made up of living beings who are led, inspired, and driven by the Holy Spirit of God. This is a creative and powerful energy that moves and transforms throughout all of humanity.

In order to survive, the church as an organization must apply many of the strategies used in corporate entities. For most congregants and leaders, this businesslike component of church management is foreign and overshadowed by some mystical illusion that God is not interested in that aspect of his church, only in spiritual matters. Many of us have fallen under the misguided premise that all you have to do is "preach and pray," and the Lord will do the rest. In some ways they are right; the Lord has indeed kept breathing life into the stumbling body of the church, despite our fumbling and mismanagement over the centuries. Nevertheless, we are called to be careful stewards of God's gifts. And therefore we the people of the church must apply sound principles of management, business, administration, and finance as we deal with the church as an organization.

Not enough seminaries or Bible institutes teach prospective pastors these concepts. Still, true leaders will find ways to become equipped with the skills and expertise of business management so they can operate their ministries with integrity. With so much information available and the technological field at our disposal, there is no room for failure.

Some may say that God has not called us to be successful but faithful. I contend, however, that he has called us to be both! If he has not called us to continue the successful mission practices of Jesus, to make the church successful, then what are we to be faithful at?

One reason proper business organization is necessary for churches is that we run ministries for which we may seek funding outside of the congregation. Many grantors, philanthropists, and other charitable donors, as well as government agencies, will grant funds only if our organizational structures are worthy of inspection and scrutiny. This foundation will prove to be the ingredient necessary to enhance the organism.

The church must evaluate the loss of finances through means of manipulation, lack of allocation, and misappropriation. If the organization is to prosper, those in both leadership and followership positions must be trained in the arts of finance, administration, organization, marketing, and stewardship! We must hold that constituency accountable for responsible stewardship practices. The lack of responsible practices presents itself as the leading cause of financial destitution, yielding to chicken dinners, fish fries, bake sales, and even waxed-

over financial impropriety. When the foundational principles of the organization are prostituted or compromised, the results are spiritual degradation, lack, and limited vision—in an institution that has been empowered by a God who owns everything, therefore without limitations! Organization merits the ability to undergo close inspection and scrutiny. Organization survives under such analysis unless some impropriety exists. Organization sets in motion clear tenets of fair and complete disclosure of all activity of its existence. A lack of organization is a clear indication that disorganization is intended or that those in leadership may not be prepared to lead. Organization is not optional; it is a must!

The organism of the church, that lively hope, is often overlooked because of an improper focus on the organization, or it is misused to deter proper focus on the organization. Sometimes when congregants are moved in the powerful presence of the organism they become honestly and submissively vulnerable to this presence, and often this spiritual high is exploited. It is at that moment that offerings are asked, gleaned, as part of the moving of this powerful organism.

The organism is the lifeblood of the church, while the organization is the backbone. The organism is the body of the living Christ, empowered by the energy of the Holy Spirit! The organism is that essence that brings a contrary and conniving heart into a right relationship with its duty.

The misunderstanding of the existence of the organism, the misdiagnosis of its importance, will most assuredly lead to poor organizational practices.

When the organism is healthy, the organization grows in every aspect with truth and integrity. How can a transformed organism participate in misallocation, misappropriation, and mismanagement and coerce others to do the same? Their fruit will evidence whatever is fixed in the hearts of the inhabitants of the church. If the church is alive and tuned to the boundaries of God's bounteous blessings, she will not concentrate on games, gimmicks, and gambling! The organism has within its essential presence a sustained survival mechanism, which by divine intervention is steadfast. It is aware of foreign invasions and pollutants and is equipped to fight the fight of faith.

A careful diagnosis of our dilemma is contained herein. If we are to change the course of the impropriety present in the church, it is imperative that the leadership and congregants come to a resolved will of embracing a stewardship germane to God's way of financing his church and kingdom and treating the inhabitants.

PART I
• • • • • • •

The Diagnosis

ONE

Toward an Understanding of the Text

It is necessary to set a foundation for the remainder of this work by providing a general exegesis of the text of Matthew 21:13. This text (Matt. 21:13) is germane to the synoptic gospels (Matthew, Mark, and Luke) and forms a parallel to Isaiah 56:7 and Jeremiah 7:11, quoted here by Jesus. Throughout each of these passages is a pattern of possession shown by our Lord. He uses the personal pronoun *my* in each. Reference is made to "my house and my name." In the Jeremiah passage, a different and stronger wording is noticed: "this house which is called by my name."

Further investigation reveals to us the nature of Jesus' anger when he came into the synagogue and found activities taking place contradictory to the nature of his name. This was to be a place dedicated to who he was and what he did. It was dear to him, and he expected only activity worthy of carrying his name and ownership.

It did not seem to matter to those in this sacred place what kind of activity went on. They had shown no real honor toward something that belonged to and was dear to someone else. This was the place he would give his life for, the place he would ordain to carry out his ministry. This was the place he would charge with showing mercy, love, and sanctuary. He was the founder, the chief executive officer,

7

and he had set some boundaries for the kind of activities that should take place in "the house of prayer."

It is interesting to note the use of the word *house* in Matthew 21:13 rather than *synagogue* or *church*. House is formed by a Greek word, *oikos*, which can be interpreted as *home*. When we grammatically analyze the word home as compared to house, a different and better perspective arises. Jesus' intent for his home was altered. He found a den of thieves in a place he founded as a house of prayer. Any person would be upset and dissatisfied to find his or her home involved in activities or conduct foreign to what a home is intended to be. We will revisit this concept later in this chapter, but first let's find out the occasion of the text.

Jesus had entered Jerusalem for the Passover feast. After all the fanfare of his entrance into Jerusalem was over, he wanted to go where most of us Christians want to go to find solace, assurance, and inspiration: the church. Passover brought a number of visitors from all over the then-known world. One of the highlights of the Passover feast was the opportunity to atone for sins. The atonement of these sins carried with it the need for sacrifices. Those visiting Jerusalem were devout believers in the law and remembered the ways of their ancestors. It was a time to celebrate that great event of the death angel passing over the homes of the Israelites as it recognized the atoning blood of a lamb in Egypt prior to their deliverance. Whether they believed in the Lord seems irrelevant. Their belief system taught them to continue this tradition as a reminder of where they had come from.

Another aspect of their belief system was that faith came by relentless obedience to the law, which compelled them to offer sacrifices for sin once a year. The weakness of this belief system was also where the strength was, in the atonement of sins. It was good to repent for the sins committed; however, their repentance was one of an outward display of piety rather than an inward transformation. They had become so devout in their rituals that the real meaning of faith in God was lost. Due to this loss the place of sanctuary was now corrupt and without manifestation of its intended existence.

Some of this same faith enjoyed the corruption because of the motive for profit and the payoffs to participate. There was no better time than the Passover, with so many people present, to capitalize on the sincerity of those who were religious and ritualistic. Temple service required provision to be made to obtain what was needed for the sacrifices. Animals, wood, oil, and other provisions were needed for the sacrifices to be offered. The money changers converted the standard Greek and Roman currency into temple currency, and a temple tax had to be paid. Sacrifices were sold to satisfy a need and make a profit in the synagogue, all in the name of religion. These events taking place at the temple corrupted a solemn place of worship into a marketplace of fraud and extortion.

All around the church, and even in the church, are those interested only in their own selfish gain and making a profit, all for the good of satisfying a personal need by misappropriation, misallocation, and intimidation in the name of Jesus!

When Jesus came into the Temple of God, his disdain for the corruption he found there was apparent. The corruption of organized religion, lacking the power of God, was an embarrassment to his name. What Jesus found was a temple in need of cleansing! What he found was an invisible priesthood and perverted temple dwellers. The priesthood was a puppet of the Roman government who shared in the dues taxation of those who came to the temple. These events were under the control of the high priest, which used this exchange as a source of extortion. It was a modern day flea market and bazaar.

Jesus' condemnation for the state of affairs found in the place he loved and would later die for caused him to quote from the Septuagint version of Isaiah 56:7 and Jeremiah 7:11: "And said unto them, 'it is written, My house shall be called a house of prayer; but ye have made it a den of thieves.'" He knew their sincerity for obeying the Old Testament writings and prophets, which would blend in with the seriousness of the worshipers arriving in Jerusalem. The ritual of celebrating the Passover would also be an opportunity to extort.

As we revisit the concept of the home, those who needed a place to be inspired, informed, transformed, loved, healed, and made whole found no hope in the temple. They found no warmth or concern, nor did they find caring in the place Jesus called home. A house is distinctly different from a home. The text renders the word house, but again the interpretation is home.

Notice that the blind and the lame came to him in the temple, after the cleansing of the temple, for healing! Jesus laid a foundational imperative. Jesus showed the purpose of the house by what he did after its cleansing! When it becomes a house of prayer, it becomes a home. When it becomes a home it will become healthy. A healthy human body will not need synthetics, makeup, or make-believe to prosper. When the house becomes a home, it will not need games, gimmicks, or gambling to survive. Where there is prayer, praise, and the power of God, there you will find the transforming presence of Jesus. Where Jesus is, you will find fulfilled promises, adequate provision, and divine protection. If Jesus is in the house the temple will be cleansed.

From this text, do you find the need for temple cleansing where you are? Do you find that more emphasis is placed on things contrary to what Jesus calls his home? Is the temple you attend representative of the name of Jesus? Are the activities germane to the nature of the God you seek? Does the money raised in your temple further the mission and ministry of the Lord Jesus Christ, or do you find the appearance of robbers and thieves?

The answers to these questions will provoke much thought. You are now confronted with the awesome task of identifying your place of worship or its affiliation as a house of prayer or a den of thieves.

TWO

The Way of the Thief

This seems such a harsh description of individuals who dwelled in the temple. Jesus stated, "You have made my house a den of thieves." To get to the heart of what Jesus meant, we must consider the term *thieves* or *thief*. The root word, from the Greek *lestes*, is interpreted as *robber* or *plunderer* (these two terms will be used interchangeably). A distinction is also made between the methods of a thief and a robber. A thief usually works unnoticed, undercover, under the guise of night, and when unexpected. A thief will strike with no clear plan in mind.

On the other hand, a robber or plunderer has a specific scheme in mind, a carefully thought out plan. Robbers carry out their plan even when noticed. They usually take advantage of whatever situation is presented to them. The robber is a master manipulator, an illusionist operating with skilled precision. The robber or plunderer just takes anything of value at a moment of want or need or simply to deprive another of their possessions or value.

Scrutiny of the word plunderer reveals something interesting. It evolves from the root word *plunder*. Out of the many definitions rendered by the Thorndike and Barnhart *World Book Dictionary*, the one suitable for our investigation can also be rendered *booty*. Booty applies particularly to things carried off and shared later by a band of cohorts.

Most of the time major robberies involve more than one person. When we consider the way of the thief operating within the bounds of the church, it is fitting how things, money, self-worth, value, relationships, and the mission are carried off by invading bandits and other robbers!

The church is a sacred institution with a clearly defined parameter of blessings or curses within and outside. When the church is understood as already having a strategic plan for success, financial and spiritual, then gimmicks, games, and gambling such as bake sales, plate sales, ticket sales, raffle sales, and false charitable requests are merely schemes of waywardness directing individuals away from the blessings of God bestowed upon an obedient people. Robbers easily invade this waywardness (take advantage of people's sincere and loyal dedication of obedience), for contained within it are impediments to proper stewardship principles and enticement to stray from these principles.

When one takes an unknown path on his or her way to a specific place, he or she is prone to be confronted by robbers lurking in the darkness of night waiting for an unsuspecting prey. When people traveled from Jerusalem to Jericho, the route was a robber's paradise. They could easily hide from those who knew where they were headed, but the great risk of robbery was unknown to them. The path of success for the church has been pioneered and the foundation laid. Straying from the path of this sure foundation places individuals and the church in danger of being robbed. The robber is like a lion on the prowl, plundering the plain in search of unaware and inattentive lunch. The robber understands, has observed, and has keenly set out to rid the owner and their followers of the flow of their value that may not be fully known to them. The robber will use a facade to disarm and desensitize the church member and entice him or her to participate in his or her own robbery. It is done in a simple fashion. The victim is not even aware that a robbery has taken place. They are aware that something has happened, and it does not seem right, but to clearly identify the culprit, how they did it, and what they did becomes too tedious of a task for the amateur investigator. The robbery is done so smoothly that it is satanic, cruel, and wicked at best.

The temple thief uses the idea that what is sold is necessary for some spiritual gain or return and that without it lack is certain to follow. This thief uses the individuals' sincerity and loyalty in giving, supporting, and participating by "stroking" them into believing that God has ordained the robbery. When confronted or questioned about the tactic or why the request is necessary, the explanation is the same: "that's the way we have always done it," or "all you have to do is be obedient to the asking, and if it is done by false pretenses, God will take care of the perpetrator." Another explanation, probably the worst of all, is the promise of a blessing from God for giving or serving above and beyond what God has required.

Once the robber plunders and gets away with it a few times, he or she then becomes desensitized to the hurt inflicted upon the victim or the robber. The temple thief, yes, even the spiritual gangster, uses this sacred institution now as his or her own private haven for thievery and perceived power. He or she can no longer psychologically feel the wrong he or she does, for it has now been justified in his or her mind. Greed has overtaken the thief, and it is done just because it can be, all in the name of Jesus.

When the victims, the people of the institution, are told that the free flow of the value or spoil is to support some needed ministry or mission, it is suspect because there is no complete and fair disclosure presented, nor is there any evidence of the mission or ministry. Something smells, at least in the minds of the victims. When the leadership feels that they have to take that which is freely given and expect people to like it, perhaps it's a good indicator that a robber is in the midst. It not only smells; it's vile. It creates the very presence of evil. When a few of the victims question why they have to be robbed, or why there is no disclosure, they are cunningly and quickly thrown off course and made to believe they are the ones in the wrong. What a travesty.

In this day of checks and balances, accountability and responsibility, why has the temple thief, robber, plunderer not been investigated, indicted, and even incarcerated? Why have the inhabitants of some in the church resorted to the actions of gangsters, embezzlers, and common thieves at the cost of losing members? What has caused secular entities who would love to see the demise of the church to question the integrity of a sacred institution? Has the movement of kingdom building been diminished to a following? Are there really payoffs and hush funds in place to keep this proverbial ball rolling? With such a lucrative institution, billions of dollars annually, can anything be done or will God have to intervene?

Be careful of unfulfilled promises of blessings. Be leery of those dressed as pious pontiffs prevaricating about the need to address someone in need. Be careful when someone takes you down an uncharted path known only to them and a select few. The possibility exists that this is only an attempt to plunder the pockets and self-worth of guilt-ridden persons or individuals who are driven by the opportunity to show how much they have or who they are!

The greatest travesty is that the very purpose of this institution called the body of Christ, the church, is polluted, watered down, and worst of all, compared to the hustle of gangbangers and drug dealing that takes place in the streets. It may seem an extreme comparison; however, when the order of the day is how much we raised, we need you to give a little more, or there is added taxation without representation or disclosure, the new Christian or sinner is led to the altar of confusion. Questions are raised, the preacher becomes suspect, the leader is watched with contempt, and people are forced to choose between staying in the church and leaving. The thief, the robber, the plunderer, however, continues to proclaim all is well, which is clearly a state of denial! All is not well. Until all within the context of the church are focused on the mission and ministry of the church from a biblical view, then all is not well. Until leaders in the church truly recognize, first, the real value of the soul of an individual and not his or her wallet; recognize, first, the real value of relationship with God and each other, and not the money; recognize, first, the real value of building community and not raping it, then all is not well!

The second part of this analysis focuses on the victim who always points the proverbial finger at church leaders and their misdoings. But when we take a closer look at the thievery that goes on in the pew each week, we can see another pollutant at work. Malachi's prophetic word poses a challenging question: "Will a man rob God?" The answer comes back emphatically: yes! "You have robbed me in tithes and offerings." When we reflect on how good God has blessed us and our lives, it causes me to ask what process takes place that will lead a person to steal from the very essence that provides his or her sustenance. I am cognizant of the fact that, yes, some people are just ignorant of the biblical principle of the tithe and the offering. Some preachers even lead their people in the concept that it is an Old Testament custom and has nothing to do with the New Testament narrative. Are the children of grace expected to accept a lesser position or standard than the people of the law? Are we expected to do less with more? In a time when we have more education, more resources, greater assets, greater salaries, and an abundance of talents, we do less. We have reduced our focus to maintenance rather than ministry. In most of our situations, there is much struggle to maintain what has been handed down by our mothers and fathers.

It is necessary to propose the existence of two problems that will be discussed in detail in a later chapter. One is clearly a misunderstanding of how to get money and what to do with it. The second is the misunderstanding of money as an economic tool rather than a spiritual medium. Our lack is not economic; it's spiritual. Several years ago my pastor in Indianapolis, Indiana, Dr. T. Garret Benjamin of New Light of the World Church, gave me a book that spoke of the spiritual concept of seed time and harvest. I was quite surprised to read within this little book how people of great wealth such as the Mellons, DuPonts, Gettys, Rockefellers, and some CEOs of major corporations used biblical principles of giving to rebound financially after going broke at some point in their journeys to success. It was a simple principle. They gave until it hurt. Every day they would just pass money out to various people. They would make this statement after each distribution: "I claim my tenfold, or hundredfold, return with good to all concerned." Whatever they claimed, they had to believe it. The principle was centered on the foundation that the return must be based upon the fact that none would have to suffer loss in order for them to receive. This keeps the principle inclusive and cyclical. Each one talked about the flow of money that did not seem to end.

Scripture is clear. It's not hocus-pocus. "Give and it shall be given unto you" (Luke 6:38). "Bring ye all the tithes into the storehouse and prove [test] me ... if I will not open up the windows of heaven, and pour you out a blessing that you will not have room enough to receive" (Mal. 3:10). That is a promise of God. Yet Christians do not believe it. These same Christians are those who are determined to lead God's church. Christians are kingdom dwellers. Kingdom dwellers follow the principles of the King of the kingdom. "How then shall they call on him in whom they have not believed?" (Rom. 10:14a). The principles contained within this sacred work are used by many corporate executives, yet the very people who are called to exemplify the essence of the principles still follow while the world leads. It seems that those called by God exemplify the ways of a thief rather than of a saved child of God, stealing from themselves. Contained within those sacred words is spiritual nutrition that fuels a vibrant marketplace of abundance. It cannot be measured with the calculator. This abundance principle cannot be contained within a stock market report. The Dow Jones Industrial Average does not possess enough analysts to bring about any kind of logic. It is a principle that only the ones sold out on this principle of God can comprehend. In the spirit realm you give to receive. In the earthly realm, for many, you take to receive! These are two different principles. The spiritual principle will work in the earthly realm, but the earthly principle doesn't seem to work in and can only pollute the spiritual realm.

The first part of this work was an attempt to bring about some diagnosis of where we are in this sacred institution called the church and what is at the core of a good thing going bad in some churches. The diagnosis is very clear to most, yet favoritism, favors, and "friend-sightedness" cause individuals to see and not see, hear and not hear. A diagnosis was necessary also to make evident the fact that the way of the temple thief is one of the most conniving and dangerous that exists. It is an impediment, a barrier, and a hindrance to the very nature and necessity of the church. It is necessary that the flawed leadership of the church consider what Jesus called a house of prayer.

Further, this continued practice says something about the followers who turn the other way and cry "I did not know this was happening," while they contribute to this system of pollutants.

In the next part we will investigate further. After a preliminary diagnosis, one must do X-rays, CAT scans, MRIs, maybe even exploratory surgery, and any other means of coming up with a good prognosis. We will attempt to answer questions posed earlier and try to find out how this institution has allowed individuals at all levels of her existence on Earth turn her into a den of thieves.

This is the basis for our dilemma and demise in the church today. Some in leadership are content to take all they can, while some in the pew are set on holding back as much as they can.

PART II

• • • • • • • •

The Prognosis

THREE

The Revival of Churchmanship

As a little boy growing up in the small town of Clarkton, North Carolina, I observed something that has stayed with me all of my life. I did not know what it meant then, but now it is clear. It was in this small town that I attended Piney Grove African Methodist Episcopal Zion (A.M.E. Zion) Church. Small town USA is a very valuable training ground for what I call churchmanship. Churchmanship can be described as the art of upholding fundamental principles of Christian and church life and passing down the integrity of that life positively, prayerfully, and powerfully. This moral ethic was exemplified by protecting the next generation from the proclivities of the present one yet struggling with striving for a pure and moral life. It was a human ethic that presented itself with a strong sense of community. Every adult was a parent to someone else's child. The entire community was one, and Sunday was the culmination of that unity. On Sunday everybody dressed up to show the children another way of success and progress. The church was the central figure of the community. It was the foundation.

We were taught respect for our elders that furthered the training from our mothers and fathers. A communal network existed between the home, the school, and the church. We used what my mother called "handles" when addressing the seniors of our community, i.e., *Mr.* and

Mrs., "no, ma'am" and "no, sir," "yes, ma'am" and "yes, sir", *please* and *thank you*. Adults were respected as elders and not as our friends. Their friendship and love came by their teaching and the examples they set for us to follow. This was churchmanship.

Regardless of the differences of opinion, mistreatment, and the like, churchmanship taught us that we reconcile, forgive, and show within our living that God truly is love! Encouragement and building up the community, church, and each other was the order of the day.

During the week people helped one another in whatever way they could. Everybody worked hard to feed their families and cared about the survival of others. It was a love ethic. Love was the preemptive motive, and servanthood was the resulting action.

What I now know experientially was taught to me some time ago. These small town farmers, teachers, preachers, and common laborers understood churchmanship. It was a principle handed down to them by their mothers, fathers, grandmothers, and grandfathers, and in turn they handed it down to us, protecting the integrity and character of the church, God, family, and community. It was a principle of maintaining a steadfast priority of God, family, and community. Churchmanship alerted us to the fact that how we treated our neighbors and our community was reflective of how we related to God. How we treated the church was reflective of our relationship with God. We were taught that what you did for your neighbors was a clear indication of your right relationship with the God of love.

I can remember times when I was growing up when the older saints in the church stopped my friends and me from playing in the church. They taught us that the church was a sacred place and reverence to God was always paramount. When we went into the pulpit area they would almost scold us, and then they taught us that place was for only the ordained of God, the preachers. We were taught that if we were in the church even for choir rehearsals or social gatherings we should maintain this reverential ethic.

This really started years before their time and mine. Israelites, although filled with all the proclivities, infirmities, and wretchedness of a stubborn and rebellious people, held in high esteem the name of

God, Yahweh, Elohim. The name of God was so precious, so revered, that only the consecrated and sanctified could handle affairs relative to that name. His word, the very mind of God, was never laid anywhere but in a sacred place.

Prior to Israel being delivered from Egyptian bondage, there was a perpetual practice of honoring their God and teaching their children to do the same. A strong sense of community was so evident that God commanded them to kill any other tribe or nation they came in contact with.

After their deliverance they began to forfeit the practice that delivered them from bondage: consistent prayer, unity in the community, and reverence for God. No longer did they teach their children the tenets of reverence for God or his word. The children now witnessed, in parents, the opposite of right nurturing. Rather than passing down examples of right living within the context of a chosen people, their children witnessed degradation in the very moral and relationship ethics they used to practice.

The name of the book Deuteronomy means "the second giving." Because of disobedience, stubbornness, and a deliberate turning from God, these chosen people wandered forty years in the wilderness until God delivered them from their suffering by killing them. Then God lifted people who would live and teach this practice of right living and obedience to the remnants, those left after those who died in the wilderness. Unlike them, this generation possessed the character and integrity of a people after the heart of God, who would pass that integrity on from generation to generation. Each time this attitude of worship, reverence, and obedience to God was overshadowed by sin and disobedience, the result was suffering, lack, fear, destruction, and then bondage of the community of Israel.

God had even set apart an entire tribe, known as the Levites, to handle his affairs on Earth. Within the context of service to God was the intimate relationship with him. Special individuals had been chosen to handle the word of God, the administration of God, and the implementation of God's will. Nothing second-best or unclean could ever be exalted in the temple of service to such a Holy God.

Persons needing to atone for sin could only go to the outer court of the temple. There they would offer their sacrifices to the priest, who in turn offered them to God. Prior to the priesthood of the believer, a time when only the priest could offer prayers to God on behalf of the people, the Lord would accept no prayer, no sacrifice, nor any offering from ordinary persons.

The temple had been built to certain specifications; the vestments of the temple had to be placed a special way and handled by special individuals. Not that there was any value to these vestments; on the contrary, the fact that they were instruments of worship to the most high made them vehicles worthy of special handling and treatment. Also, the priesthood rather than the priest was the focal point of this service.

The temple was the place of gathering or assembly where the presence of God was experienced and realized. It was his home! This institution represented a peculiar plan and purpose for chosen individuals specializing in service to a just and holy God. His presence was such that his reality was not taken for granted but was experienced in the day–to-day life of the believer. The word of God had to be handled carefully and rightly. Although the priest did his job, the people failed after each prayer of atonement. Eventually God would get tired of their outward expressions of worship.

Those who knew him understood the "reverential awe" relative to his name. He could only be spoken of as supreme. His word was, and is, who he is. To speak of God blasphemously would be to speak of all his self-existence in the same derogatory way. Therefore careful mention of anything of God would always be done with spiritual integrity and holy order. The temple was entered with a posture proportionate to perpetual piety. The seriousness of the people of God and their commitment to upholding the essence of who God was, why he was, and where he was verifies the unconditional promise, protection, and provision encompassed in that essence.

God promised he would protect them and provide for them if they would walk with him, serve him, and live in him all the days of their lives. In the people of God and their walk with him there was a direct correlation between the total immersion in God's will and the rewards and the mere religious ritual assent to that will and the lack of rewards. When victory was realized, Israel seemed to always be in the direct will and ways of the Lord! On the other hand, when defeat overtook them, there always appeared to be a deviation from that will. When the life of his people was recognized as belonging to the God who made them, their presence was easily recognizable. This recognition was not in their weaknesses, faults, or shortcomings, but in the representation of the God who made them, a people representative of the God who created them. Spiritual integrity was the order of the day. Their existence in God mirrored kingdom dwelling. This is not to say that ordinary life was not experienced—quite the contrary. Even in their day-to-day living they were identified as the people of God. This example was not one of perfection but of protection. Nothing they did or said was to cause others to stumble. While protecting their own proclivities, unworthiness, and unrighteousness before the world, it was imperative to also protect the name and nature of God. As he molded, fixed, shaped, and filled them, he also emptied them, daily, of those same infirmities of flesh.

The transference of this salvific benefit is encompassed in the glorious exchange that took place in the process of living for our time. Jesus would impute his righteousness to our unrighteousness and his sinlessness to our sinfulness. The doctrine of imputation means to give credit to something or someone who does not deserve nor merit the credit. It is worthy of mention that this was not based on our perfect state of being nor on our works. To pretend to be perfect or sinless is hypocritical. But to recognize our individual shortcomings and to insulate them with God's grace is to exalt his mercy and riches not our own. This is churchmanship! It is a standard rooted solely in the grace and mercy of God. A group of baptized believers recognizing that grace has brought them safe thus far and grace will complete the journey is churchmanship. It is not hunting for and exploiting faults in others by tearing them down or constantly reminding them of those faults. It is that recognized variable that "all have sinned and come short of the glory of God" (Rom. 3:23). This suggests that sin is not past tense but perpetual.

Churchmanship does not look upon the change of one's nature, but the change of one's position, one's standing before a just and loving God. Most Christians realize that sin is all around them. Contained within that body is not perfection but forgiveness. Because of the gift of grace bestowed upon this body of imperfect beings, reverence for the one who saves, forgives, and delivers is paramount. Churchmanship recognizes the inclusiveness of all within the body as partakers of the divine benefit. It is the reverence that warrants integrity. It is the nature of the purpose of the church purchased by the sacrificial blood of the lamb that calls us to a standard of behavior. It calls us to view the cross of Calvary and to carry its burden, to carry its banner in our witness. Churchmanship sees us as we are, yet it compels us to strive toward what we should become in Christ Jesus! Perhaps the most significant aspect of this guiding of individuals toward what they can and should become is the recognition that the persons pushing shield their own shortcomings, protecting those they push by insulating them and keeping their focus on the prize rather than the proclivity.

When the body of Christ loses sight of the ingredients of her nature, when the standard of churchmanship is invaded by exclusivity, a spiritual demise takes place. As we look to the horizon of churchmanship and the church, can we recognize the demise of spiritual integrity? Can we see or do we just look the other way when we recognize this peripheral pollutant invading the fiber of confession of faith? The compromise of a spiritual and cultural standard lends blame to all involved.

My nurturing in the church developed from this tradition. Today people do not hold the pastorate in the same high esteem as they once did. Scandal after scandal has injected viruses into the esteem of the pastorate. When one minister falls, society blames and includes all ministers. When one church splits, society, both sacred and secular, blames and places all churches in the same vain. The root cause is the demise of churchmanship. There are many symptoms but one cause.

Today, within the context of my own experience, there is much turning on one another and not enough turning to one another. Individual achievements are tools that equip the individuals within the kingdom of God to serve more effectively. Achievement is not a tool of selfish motive and self service, but of service to the least of God's children. Whatever a person's level of success or lack thereof, they have been equipped by God for service in the kingdom. The kingdom of God is where God rules. Today those in the kingdom seem to have forgotten the principle of following the mandates of the King: love one another; bear the burdens of one another; share with one another; forgive one another; encourage one another; provide for one another; get along with one another. Churchmanship is also defined by Acts 2:42–47: "And they continued steadfast in the apostles' doctrine and fellowship, and in breaking of bread, and in prayers. And fear came upon every soul; and many wonders and signs were done by the apostles. And all that believed were together, and had all things common; and sold their possessions and goods, and parted them to all men as every man had need. And they, continuing daily with one accord in the temple, and breaking bread from house to house, did eat their meat with gladness and singleness of heart, praising God, and having favor with all the people. And the Lord added to the church daily such as was being saved." This is the practical application of a love principle within family, church, and community.

The pulpit and the pew, in many instances, seem to be used now for props and promptings of showcasing dress and style, who has the greater following, and who can do it better than the other. Of course, you also have the power and money hustling. Don't misunderstand me; money is a necessary tool. It's not the money that is the problem. It is the love of it that leads people to greed and power brokering.

Today anybody who has felt an urge to preach can enter the holy of holies without any regard to the call of God. Today defections from mainline denominations that many startups have grown from find that those who once graced their pews now condemn the foundation they came from. These defectors view their defection as a direct command from God to challenge the truths of traditional churchmanship as they promote division while embracing a more contemporary style. True churchmanship, as I experienced it, embraced both. People within the same community shared with the Baptists on the second and fourth Sundays and with the Methodists on the first and third Sundays. Whatever needs arose within the community or church was borne by both churches. This is true churchmanship.

There is a place for diversity, and being different does not mean being divisive. Today division is apparent between and within denominations. There is no such thing as nondenominational. According to the *Wycliffe Dictionary of Theology*, the definition of denomination is a class, kind, or sort designated by a specific name; ecclesiastically, a body or sect holding peculiar distinctions. Churchmanship recognizes the diversity of all ecclesiastical bodies, although doctrine may differ.

The focus today has become so much on the doctrinal differences within the bodies of religious institutions that the right effect for change, for altering blighted human conditions within communities, and for enhancing networking relationships is lost in the maze of this ongoing debate of who is right. The needs of humanity are much more important. We see a strong commercial religion that produces billions of dollars annually, yet many are still hungry, homeless, and stare in the face of hopelessness daily. I am not saying that the church alone is responsible for solving this crisis. However, the church must do a lot more to aid in solving the crisis in light of some of the pleas for money without some of those in need ever seeing the money or aid.

The church is intrinsic within the life of the community. It should not be viewed as a separate entity but as the spiritual foundational force of the community that everything else is built around. The demise in spiritual integrity arises out of forces surrounding and within the church pronouncing that it is a separate institution and should remain so. These forces have an agenda that exalts the theme that the church today is not a necessary entity. Sadly, some within the church see an opportunity to capitalize on the riches produced, as a result of this personal agenda, with a sense of urgency. There is a sense of urgency because the door is being shut.

Spiritual integrity is important to all who claim salvation, Christianity, or churchmanship if we are to maintain a positive and transferable integrity of imitating what one confesses and professes. The leadership sets the standard. Leadership must be concerned about the integrity of God and how people come to know God, as seen through the faith walk and practice of the leader. In secular society an organization takes on the tenor of the leader. Caring, positive, powerful, and prayerful leadership in the church is churchmanship.

In many cases what is seen at different levels of leadership may be interpreted as something other than integrity—certainly something other than churchmanship. These leaders, both clergy and lay, hide behind facades of suspicion. While participating in that which is suspect, the demise brings with it apathy from the remaining body that cries out "they are going to do what they want anyway." What a tragedy! This leads many followers to believe that there is no integrity in the ranks of leadership anymore. The unfortunate result is people leave the church. But "all is well." Certainly in the church I grew up in people did not see integrity or churchmanship as an option but as a necessary ingredient, a way of church life.

It is incumbent upon all who subscribe to the notion of spirituality, Christianity, and churchmanship to investigate, enlist, and involve that inward despair of incentive, compelling us to revive the tradition of church standard. It is more than a following, but a movement. It is a clear indication that we, the silent majority, have lost concern for inclusive and thriving churchmanship when we focus on followers rather than disciples. Who shall we point to for a lack of this proper focus and who shall we point to when reclaiming and renewing this needed ingredient?

It is obvious that those who have this swelling tide of desire to see the church at her best, engulfed with the flow of Christocentric benefit, must lead the revival. Everything is ready and in place for the serious student of church life and progress to stand now for the rich heritage handed down to us for many generations. It is a rich heritage that compels us to be mindful of our past, for it is our foundation. It is a heritage that compels us to hallow our present, for these are the best of times. It is a heritage that compels us to embrace with hope and faith our future, for it is truly bright. And if it seems to you that the time is not now, then when? If it seems to you that you are not the person to revive the integrity and churchmanship of this institution called the church, then who will do it? If it seems to you that it is not to be done where you are, then where shall the revival begin?

This inward zeal cannot be taught in seminary or any other institution of higher learning. It is an innate quality. It is a quality borne out of a spiritual integrity. I know I am not the only one with this quality. I know I am not the only one who knows this truth. I know I am not the only one who longs for the kind of churchmanship instilled in many of us. I know I am not the only one who feels somebody should say and do something about this demise. But perhaps there are only a few, like me, courageous enough to do so. The burden is within you; you cannot transfer the task to someone else. Blow the trumpet In Zion!

FOUR

The Pastor, Prostitution, and Power

What was once a noble calling, a respected position within the church body and surrounding community, has now, in many instances, become suspect. With the emergence of ministry scandals and a media bent intensely on exploiting the worst in the leaders of such ministries, it is not surprising that pastoral ministry has become questionable in the sight of churchgoers and would-be Christians.

Did God know what these times would bring for the promulgators of the gospel he would call them to proclaim? What is the pastor's responsibility? What does the pastor do when his or her loyalty to the one who called him or her becomes diluted, misplaced, or compromised? As a pastor of twenty-two years, I have found myself wrestling with the answers to these questions many times. It would seem that now, more than before, a pastor must ensure that his or her calling is certain. It is not a time for self-indulgence or self-serving motives.

The call to become a pastor is distinctly different from the call to preach! Pastoring is leading, tending, teaching, developing relationships, and disciplining those of a particular sheepfold or congregation. Although an essential essence of ministry, preaching is proclaiming the written word of truth. The pastor must be free to hear the voice of God guiding him or her through the maze of contentious memberships, in-

31

competent leadership, and imposing hardships. To pastor is to follow a divine purpose! It is an appointed position solely authenticated by the appointer, God. Where the pastor is appointed by someone other than God, loyalty is divided; in some cases it is imposed, while in others the pastor chooses his or her own object of loyalty.

It is within the context of this medium that a pastor must choose wisely and prayerfully those who are worthy of receiving his or her loyalty and dedication. One will find himself pandering at the pool of popularity when the choice is based on elevation rather than election.

It is necessary to state a poignant point as to my position on the pastor. There is no nobler calling. There is no other individual, anywhere, who is more tenacious, caring, bold, obedient, faithful, conscientious, astute, intelligent, studious, visible, blessed, or giving. All these tremendous attributes are in addition to the fact there is no other individual, anywhere, who is more blamed, lonely, falsely accused, picked out, picked on, criticized, stressed, depressed, expressed, oppressed, squeezed, or thankless. The pastor is divinely called to juggle the inward struggle, often manifested in a way contrary to that turmoil. Much of these struggles are imposed by external forces; however, there are self-inflicted wounds that pastors bring upon themselves through the mediums of spiritual prostitution and power plays. Spiritual prostitution is the act of subordinating or selling one's divinely appointed authority and assignment for a lesser status and presenting that lesser status as gain. It is no secret that most of us called by God to this awesome task would have rather passed it on to someone else. It is a journey like no other journey, from the abode of heaven to the depths of hell. It is a journey that only God and another pastor can understand. To be chosen by God is not to be taken lightly. When a pastor makes careful inventory and assessment and realizes he or she has been touched by the master himself, running and hiding is an inviting force. To stand in that calling presupposes divine enabling!

When the pastor resolves within his or her own mind that the call is not superior to the internal wrestling, spiritual prostitution has been committed. This is a self-imposed infliction that results in excuse rendering. No one else has to blame you, nor have they accused you of inconsistencies; it is just something that finds its way to you. It is a feeling of inadequacy that one places upon oneself. God has nothing to do with it. This is self-imposed prostitution, which is perhaps the worst kind. Selling oneself short of a clearly defined destiny is nothing less than a tragedy. Oftentimes this prostitution of one's self is a defection from a greater posture that God has placed us in to a lesser position, but one that has the appearance of greater attraction. This is a dangerous place to be. This place lends strength to those who seek to destroy the pastor. It is a place that creates and feeds sinful appetites. It is where pastors fall into "diver's temptations"—(various attractive temptations). Self-inflicted spiritual prostitution is alive and well. There are a tremendous number of talented and called pastors who subordinate that talent to bona fide spiritual pimps at prices they cannot afford. This in no way is antiauthority, but a call to those in authority to understand that leadership plus authority equals servanthood, and servanthood is at the very core of the pastoral call.

A second type of spiritual prostitution is the act of seeking an unappointed, unordained position with no qualification for the sole purpose of obtaining some unearned financial gain or an unwarranted favor, all at the price of the pulpit and the price of the call to that pulpit. Spiritual prostitution raises its selfish head at that point of congregational exploitation and sacrifice, when the priority of the current pulpiteer is another bigger or "better" pulpit because of mere desire rather than merit. It becomes evil and breaks a vow of comrade trust when another pastor and family are hurt because of such greed or power brokering.

The Lord hath said, "I will never leave you nor forsake you" (Deut. 31:6, 8). However, there comes a time in all of our lives when it seems that the Lord and everybody else have left us alone. This is a very vulnerable time of testing and trial, of self-criticism and self-analysis. It can also be a time of depression and denial. It is at this time that one can easily develop wrong attitudes toward oneself, one's calling, and God. It is a time of thanklessness and ungratefulness from others and a time of loneliness and selfishness from within. A semblance of purpose is lost, and the result is resorting to something lesser than what we are or where God wants us. This perhaps is the greatest contributing fac-

33

tor toward submitting the pulpit to less than the divine prerogative it possesses.

Attorneys have a sacred trust bond, law enforcement officers have a fraternal bond, and other professionals have similar bonds. The pastor, in the context of my vantage point, oftentimes is hurt, betrayed, or detained by another pastor or minister, regardless of the level or office of the inflicting pastor. From where I serve, pastors are often called upon to support some financial asking, without disclosure, and when that pastor refuses or asks for disclosure, he or she is said to be antagonistic, unsupportive, or against the program. Another example is when pastors come together to discuss what can be done about some of the improprieties that occur, only to have one power broker his or her way into the leadership's realm by disclosing what was said at the table of brotherhood. The power brokering is more vicious when the pulpit sought brings great benefits. There have even been situations in which a pastor's struggle came from simply being different or diverse but perceived as divisive. This false perception or envious spirit has resulted in a pastor's livelihood being jeopardized.

This is a time of opportunistic misfortunes within the body of Christ. One would think that in the body of Christ there would be a call to arms of all Christian soldiers, particularly among pastors, to battle the external forces and powers that be. Quite the contrary! Scanning the horizon of Christendom, one finds more power struggles within the body (pastors against pastors) than from external sources.

Admittedly, although some may say this is a bit overboard, this behavior is somewhat satanic in nature. This may also seem to be a harsh statement, but the Scriptures are clear: "'The thief cometh not, but to steal, and to kill, and to destroy: I am come that they might have life and that they may have it more abundantly'" (John 10:10). When an individual sets out to kill a person's ability for life, liberty, and the pursuit of happiness; when an individual sets out to steal a person's stability and peace of mind; when another individual sets out to destroy a person's character or integrity, that is evil and wicked, both of which come from satanic influence. In the body of Christ, we are to edify, which means to build up, not tear down, regardless of the justification. Power brokering promotes division and creates an atmosphere of spiritual prostitution and posturing. The Scriptures are clear in pronouncing that there is strength in unity and that this unity is the foundation by which the integrity of the pulpit is maintained (Eph. 4:3–7, 11-13) "Endeavoring to keep the unity of the Spirit in the bond of peace. There is one body and one Spirit, even as ye are called in one hope of your calling. One Lord, one faith one baptism, One God and Father of all who is above all, and through all, and in you all. But unto every one of us is given grace according to the measure of the gift of Christ. And he gave some apostles; and some, prophets; and some, evangelists; and some, pastors and teachers; For the perfecting of the saints, for the work of the ministry, for the edifying of the body of Christ; Till we all come in the unity of the faith, and of the knowledge of the Son of God, unto a perfect man, unto the measure of the stature of the fullness of Christ."

When God's provision points to the inevitable fact that there is enough for everybody, one can rest in and rely on the fact that if he called you, he will provide for you. When this poignant fact is lost in the midst of favoritism, turfs, unmerited elevation rather than divine election, and sellouts to the highest bidders, the church becomes a red-light district, and the sacred call to pastor is reduced to something other than a divine calling of God.

How does one bestowed with the divine call and election of God subordinate to a lesser degree of service? The acceptance of the call of God brings with it an attraction that is so magnetic that it not only draws others, but it also draws satanic forces that seem to be summoned to do nothing more than discourage, demean, damage, and destroy. This battle becomes internalized and tugs at the very fiber of the servant's faith, joy, and steadfastness.

Perhaps the next characteristic of how this subordinated power brokering can take place is often overlooked because of its appearance, and that is that some may not have ever been called to the position of pastor. It is obvious in Scripture that where and when God plants his servants, results take place, progress is proven, and fruit bearing is realized. Some pastors and layfolk are merely plants for personal and political agendas, posturing as servants, but are no more than hirelings waiting for the highest wage offering. They can be planted by false presentation of the self or by some higher official who has offered pay-offs for special favors in return.

I must be careful here, for I do not want to be guilty of making un-proven prevarications or accusations. I do not in any way imply that some high-level pontiffs within the body of Christ have sent prophets to pulpits simply to support their greed. However, I will state cate-gorically that the evidence is strong within some denominations. Why would the cause of Christ ask the church to be prostituted, polluted, polarized, and plundered for the sake of personal gain? The pastors of these churches are there for no other purpose, and some congregants are party to it. The overwhelming damage comes in the form of broken congregations and stained dimensions of the body of Christ. Although unaware at the time, pastors are bruised in their ministries for years. Often overlooked is the profound fact that whatever you do to get to a particular pulpit or position, you must also maintain that posture to stay there! When this disdained ploy is confronted with the divine providence and imperative of God, one is brought to a polemic—re-pentance or death!

The perception is that when you give favor to those in power, power is then shared with you. Nothing can be further from the truth. Absolute power is selfish. Those hungry for power will create allies to gain that power, but when the allies want their share of it, power is then corrupted and becomes selfish. Those who surrendered their call, their election, for this perceived sharing of power, are now brought to a place of personal powerlessness. The spiritual integrity of the call is now compromised. The position of authority is prostituted, and the people perish. The Scriptures verify this point in Proverbs 29:18a: "where there is no vision, the people perish: but he that keepeth the law, happy is he." Interpreted, this would mean where there is no pro-phetic revelation, the people cast off restraints. The church then only experiences ritualistic pomp and circumstance with no real presence, praise, or power of God! It is a very dangerous posture to take. It will cost you more than you want to pay, keep you in a place of lack longer than you want to stay, and put you on public display. Even worse, you will end up somewhere other than under the divine protection of God.

The conclusion is that there is no higher calling for the local church than the office of pastor. The bishop, the district superintendent, presiding elder, or supervisor has no greater anointing for the progress of that local church than the call to pastor. When you consider the biblical hermeneutic, all the other positions are outgrowths of the noble call to pastor. They are simply positions of greater service, not postures of intimidation, and should not be used to compromise the pastor or his or her position. They are positions that render service and support to the call of the pastor at the local church level. If those positions, though of a high and noble office, are used to place unwarranted stress, whether through financial, social, or governmental means, upon the local church or pastor, then they are out of character and certainly do not conform to Scripture. Any position at any level that stands as a diluting agent infiltrating the authority of the pastor is satanic and warrants repentance or excommunication.

If the structure of the denomination within the parameters of its polity presents itself as a detainee or hindrance of the work of the pastor at the local church level, that structure is worthy of analysis and correction. I understand that statements such as the previous ones border the words uttered by non-traditionalists and reformers prior to the Reformation. Speaking out against years of tradition does not indicate that the writer is against tradition, but merely against traditions that are unfounded in the biblical sense of what forms our motive. Any compromise of the authority of the pastor at the local church level by any entity dilutes, detains, deters, dissociates, and destroys the level of authentic pastoral leadership and lends credence to subordinates stepping out of the order of the chain of command. It also leads to disloyalty to God, pastor, church, and community.

A popular notion among the lay leadership of some churches is that they can usurp the authority of the pastor by appealing to his or her superior. When that superior lends credence to that process, especially when the pastor has not been given the opportunity to address the concern, it promotes disunity and disloyalty within that body. Much of this type of fraternizing is done, unfortunately, because of political posturing and pastoral disrespect. I will elaborate on this matter of lay leadership relative to pastoral leadership and authority in the next chapter. This does not in any way make an attempt to do away with the appellate rights of any level in the church; however, it does uphold the God-given rights of the position of pastor. Further, it calls to the attention of all that the pastoral position should not be compromised or prostituted for the sake of personal financial gain, power plays, or political maneuvering. What is of significant importance is that all our enabling is encompassed in our calling, and there is no need for anyone to try and destroy another.

God gives the pastor power and authority to carry out the function of the calling. Let me testify of this authority. I took very seriously the call of God upon my life after running from him for eight long and tedious years. I was in my office in Fayetteville, North Carolina, when the phone rang. What appeared to me to be a woman clearly deranged or drunk turned out to be the phone call that changed my life. The woman on the other end asked to speak with someone not affiliated with my office. I proceeded to tell her that she had the wrong number. She had tried to persuade me to come to her home for a prayer meeting and Bible study. Again I tried to get her off the phone. With a failing business, after a frustrating day, a Bible study was the last thing I was interested in. She then stated she had a word for me from the Lord. The words convicted me, so I ended up going to her home that night. She said, "'Seek ye first the kingdom of God, and his righteousness; and all these things shall be added unto you' [Matt. 6:33]. The Lord wants you to know that, brother Neill!" What an awesome revelation—one that was needed in my life at that time. I knew immediately that this had to be a direct and divine admonition from God. It was that conviction in my heart that reinforced that I had been truly called by God for his service.

Remember, my friend, when you heard the call for the first time? Remember how you were going to set things right for God? You were going to do his will regardless of what came your way. From that

Tuesday night in December of 1986 until now, I have tried to maintain my faithfulness to the integrity of his call upon my life. I have missed many financial and promotional opportunities but not at the risk of the integrity of the call of God. I have not been included in the inner circle of power dealings and brokering, which would have landed me thousands of dollars, maybe even millions in my lifetime. I have not found favor with my superiors. I have not paid for any position, nor have I brokered or hurt any other individual for the same. Praise God! When I was in school and trying to maintain a family and business, I remained faithful. Once I was told by my boss that I had to work on Sunday. I simply said to him, "I will be in the pulpit on Sunday. If my job is terminated because of my stance, call me so I won't waste a trip." You know God returned the faithfulness back to me. I would rather have authority than power! For power without authority is powerlessness! I would rather have favor over popularity!

If you find that you have compromised with your call for the sake of becoming a popular force, let me offer a bit of spiritual advice. God has not forgotten his call upon your life. If you are alive you have an opportunity to make it right. One pleasing reminder about God: he will give us time to get it right. Through all of our wrestling, he is still molding us into becoming that which he has predestined and ordained. It is always more attractive to go the road of popularity and perceived power than the one of suffering and divine election. I have learned (and am still learning) and resolved within myself to stay with the Lord. Conform only to his will. That does not mean you disrespect authority or become arrogant. In the words of Jesus, "he that exalts himself shall be abased; and he that shall humble himself shall be exalted" (Luke 14:11). God bless you, servant of God! May he who hath called you with a holy calling keep you, strengthen you, be merciful unto you, give you peace, and cause his face to shine upon you!

FIVE

Spiritual Pollutants and the Perishing Pew

Perhaps the most damaging effect of wayfaring leadership and blind followership is the birth of pollutants stagnant within the body of Christ. The reason this problem is both pastoral and lay is found in Proverbs 29:18a: "Where there is no vision, the people perish." This means that where there is no prophetic revelation the people cast off restraints. When the prophet does not give right revelation of the truth of God's word, the hearer will not have the proper standard by which to measure a right behavior. Right behavior usually leads to right actions. Take for example a basketball team that has superstars but no real knowledge of the fundamentals of the game. A team with fewer superstars but fundamental soundness will pose a problem for the team of superstars. Soon the team of superstars will fall behind and pollutants will set in. Their attitude is they are better, more talented, and should not have a problem beating the other team. But now they are behind and cannot understand why they are being beaten by a team they feel is inferior. The pollutants are now interfering with their game. They begin arguing with each other, and a team game now becomes individual play. They fall further and further behind. The coach cannot seem to get through to them that they must play fundamental ball. At the buzzer at the end of the game they finally realize that they do

40

not know any fundamentals. They have not been trained in the art of fundamental playing. Whose fault is it? Well, the responsibility is shared by the parents, the players, and the coaches. They all have some responsibility to prepare themselves with principles to guard against the pollution they face in the world.

Pollutants are always unwelcome agents. They stain that which is good or becoming so. Pollutants have ingredients that change the composition of anything they invade. When preventative measures are not in place, pollutants have easy access to a desired target. When undetected, pollutants linger. When pollutants are detected, countermeasures must be implemented to rid the entity of the unwanted disease. It can invade in many ways unknown to its victim.

Our discussion focuses on the "spiritual pollutants" that invade the spiritual growth and development of the body of Christ, although the principle of invasion is the same, corporately and individually. Broadly speaking, spiritual pollutants are anything or anyone that impedes the spiritual progression of the people of God toward the will of God. A pollutant is anything or anyone that causes the invasion of impure viruses in the body, bringing about a physical, chemical, or in our case a spiritual change different than that once present, bringing about harm.

This spiritual progression is the foundation essential for all other progress. Hindrances distract the Christian from a successful faith walk. One may ask just what that walk is. Careful analysis and perusal of the biblical narrative will reveal that God has always set parameters for his people. As an earthly father or mother sets guidelines for his or her children with rewards for obedience and punishment for disobeying, God has also given us a set of prescribed boundaries that, adhered to, will reward us, and disobeyed, will punish us. The punishment does not come from God but from our own disobedient actions that create an impeded and successful faith walk. Fathers and mothers desire to see their children succeed in every area of life. God has also made certain promises to his children, provisions to achieve those promises, and protections until the promises are realized.

There are key dynamics to this faith walk with God. First, the operative word and the key is *faith!* Hebrews 12:6–7 declares, "Without faith it is impossible to please God; they that come to him must first believe that he is, and that he is a rewarder of them that diligently seek him." Faith is not foolishness but factual reality. When the Christians faith becomes faulty, the obvious cause is the presence of some pollutant that permeates the very fiber of that faith fact. The Bible seems to indicate that faith is progressive, seeking some predetermined goal. When the proper faith walk is acquired, pollutants will become faith enhancers rather than mere obstacles. Without this faith walk, pollutants are insurmountable obstacles. These pollutants inject impurities and dirt that cloud clear vision and a clear understanding of what God's intent is, where his intent is, and why it is. Faith is a preventative measure counteracting the composition of most pollutants. Yet there are some pollutants that even faith will strive stressfully to eliminate. This poignant fact brings me to the second point.

When faith is based on circumstances rather than trust in God, the walls of protection are weakened and pollutants present themselves. It is difficult to walk in faith when one is sitting still or looking back while trying to move forward. There is a faith that looks backward, however, which is a reflective look. It looks at prior circumstances that were overcome. When David was given every excuse to run from what seemed insurmountable odds (1 Sam. 17), his faith involved immediate recall, a reflection on past danger and deliverance from that danger through divine enabling. His faith did not cause retreat but reinforced the commitment to rid himself of the obstacle.

Faith in our circumstances reduces us to relying on our condition in the circumstances. When you are faced with a situation with seemingly no way out, you could simple hope that it goes away—that's faith in your condition or circumstances—or you can rely on faith that you can move out of that situation or move the situation—that's true faith. Faith in our condition or circumstances is pollutant-enhancing faith. It takes us to a place that keeps us relying on the circumstances to just go away! Faith in God brings us to the calm assurance that our previous experience of trial was met with victory. I don't know how; I just know that whatever I was experiencing, I could do very little about it.

I also realized that at that point of my weakness and inadequacy, God became the faith fact I needed to stay on course. The concept of faith is rooted in the fact of God: what he is, who he is, what he has, and what he can do as no other God can, on my behalf.

In this section we will discuss and identify three key spiritual pollutants that the discerning person can easily recognize. Consider the following:

1. Biblical and administrative illiteracy is growing.

At the very core of our dilemma are biblical illiteracy and the lack of knowledge of how to administer the word of God. The fact of God is found in the Bible. What and who he is, what he thinks, his nature, how he feels, his relationship with his people, his infinite beginning and end are all contextually contained in him and revealed in his word. It is true that one can realize God through the method of natural or general revelation. That is the revelation of God through nature, history, and God's image in mankind. However, a greater revelation is through the method of supernatural or special revelation, which is direct communication from God. The Scriptures are a clear method of knowing and understanding God. The word of God is the thoughts of God, the God-breathed word through the writer, not the writer's own interpretation. The pew dweller is perishing for lack of this revelation. The lack of serious biblical study yields spiritual pollutants that hinder the growth of the body of Christ. When the focus is balancing of the budget, raising assessments, who the next pastor will be, unfair taxation, incomplete and improper financial disclosure, selfish and greed-ridden leadership, and a willful ignorance coupled with a lack of desire to participate, the clear cause is a body polluted and perishing.

The ultimate achievement for the Christian is to know God. When individuals within the church know God, and he is able to possess their hearts, he will also possess the essence of their desire to grow in and please him. The desire to know and please God creates barriers for pollutants and incentives to strive toward the prize of Christ. Since Jesus established the church and the means by which the church would function and succeed, we would do well to understand that revelation in our attempts to lead, both as clergy and laypersons. The church suffers from polluted leadership in both ranks. At the core of that pollution are uninformed and ill-equipped individuals seeking the glory and glamour of leadership with little or no preparation for it. In the past one's status within a given community or background in a highly visible secular profession has been the main criteria necessary to serve in the house of God. But every person seeking service within the church should be reminded that the internal call to ministry is coupled with the external call to preparation. We must be called by God to serve in the spiritual service of God. After the call is sure, we then must be trained for the specific service God has gifted us for internally. The call and the preparation go hand in hand and do not contradict but complement each other.

What is the cause of the demise of interest in and attendance at Sunday church schools, Bible studies, or any credible teaching ministry at a given church, particularly in mainline churches? Why would those who profess the call of God feel that training is not necessary for that divine journey of service? Several reasons come to mind. Perhaps the leading reason is the lack of commitment by the parishioner. From my vantage point, two of the least attended sessions in the church are Sunday school and Bible study. Special workshops are a close third. As I travel within my own denomination, visit other churches, and converse with colleagues of various persuasions, the conclusion seems to cross denominational lines: there is a deep concern for training leaders in the church, both clergy and laypersons. When people in leadership positions have little or no clue as to what they should do or why, this creates a foundation for invading viruses.

This principle can be applied to secular organizations as well as sacred. However, it is more prevalent in a church setting. This in no way implies that those in church leadership are less intelligent than those in secular leadership. For some reason there is a philosophy in the church that God has not called them to be successful, just faithful. Some feel it is not necessary to run the organizational aspect of the church with business management principles, but just to be faithful. So there isn't any need to be trained in marketing, management, administration, and the like; just be faithful in whatever position you're in, and things will work out somehow.

Another cause of the demise of commitment to training is the lack of confidence in the leader's teaching ability or knowledge of the subject matter. Does this mean that every pastor or Bible study teacher must attend seminary? Of course not. It would be great, but the teacher must be equipped to teach by both studious astuteness and divine anointing. You cannot substitute one for the other; both are necessary. One's avocation of teaching does not substitute for one's vocation. There must be the call (vocation) to teach and the preparation (avocation). When a person has an avocation, it focuses on their secular career and training for the same. The vocation of a person is their calling to do a specific task they have been divinely equipped for within the body of Christ. For example, a pastor is divinely called by God to shepherd a particular congregation. This is his or her vocation. He or she may also work as an accountant, which is his or her avocation. Paul's attempt to teach the Ephesians' church of the functional gifts requisite of a New Testament church (Eph. 4:11) allows us to know that the pastor/teacher is the correct interpretation of that text because of the absence of the conjunction in the Greek language. A pastor must be able to teach.

Still another reason for the demise of interest in and attendance at teaching settings is that the human psyche is such that people feel embarrassed when their lack of biblical knowledge is exposed. They want to know and want everyone around them to feel that they know. Anybody or anything that unveils that lack of knowledge is seen as a threat to a person's comfort zone of ignorance. That's why leaders must be equipped to teach, although the tenor of the Bible study should be one that says not knowing is all right; that is why it's called study.

A fourth leading reason for the demise of interest in learning in the church is the lack of a relevant curriculum. Does the teaching material speak to what the student is confronted with each day? Does that material suggest solutions to the dilemmas faced by the student? Does the material challenge the student to search the Scriptures? Does the teaching material present the student with definitive outcomes and objectives? These are some of the questions that address the relevance of Bible study. There are those who believe that just showing up and reading a few verses of Scripture is study. No, no; there must be a relevant curriculum that addresses not only where we go when we die, but how we live prior to our departure from Earth.

Some other reasons for the demise in attendance at the instructional setting are:

A. The time offered is not convenient or the session is too long.

B. The room or facility is not adequately lit or conducive to study.

C. There are no pertinent visual aids or other equipment to enhance the teaching.

D. Only a one-dimensional method of teaching is used.

These can be a deterrent to the teaching ministry. For many situations, real solutions have not been realized, and thus pollutants are present.

Perhaps the greatest of all the pollutants is the willful desire to remain ignorant. It may be acceptable not to know, but there is no excuse for not wanting to learn. There are those who believe that not knowing will somehow bid them excused from the task of doing.

2. The second key spiritual pollutant is <u>timid leadership</u>.

As a pastor for twenty-two years, I've experienced moments when I had been beaten up so badly that apathy became the order of the day. The art of questioning my purpose in ministry would often overtake my conviction to the call. It is at those times that one should press on rather than succumbing to the victim syndrome. I have pondered the twofold concept of whether a pastor should show weakness to the congregation and allow them to see the emotional aspects of what a prisoner of the Lord experiences or always show strength regardless of his or her situation. Perhaps there are many schools of thought on this matter; however, I find that a leader must be careful that the position of leadership or the office he or she holds is not brought to a level of disrespect or suspicion. Personally, I do subscribe to the notion that one must maintain the integrity of the office he or she holds at all costs.

Not only is one's own reputation or personal constitution at stake, but the reputations of all others in that same position, the reputation of the body of Christ, and the reputation of God are at stake.

I hasten to state that at these moments colleagues must comfort and encourage one another. However, in a structured denominational setting or hierarchy, there exists the threat of being dethroned by one's own colleagues. Everything rises or falls on leadership. When leadership is not free to hear and heed the instruction of God, it is a polluted leadership. Within the context of the hierarchical structure, gifted and envisioned leadership is welcomed and necessary. However, when that leadership is reduced to selfish agendas and motives, it is a dangerous and polluted leadership. For example, when an episcopal or hierarchical structure is in place, that leadership sets the tenor for the hierarchy. When that leadership has at the core of its intent personal and selfish greed, that leadership can and does misuse the office or authority it holds. Undue influence is placed upon those seeking advancement without qualification. Those who will not submit to undue coercion are often hurt or damaged in some way, leading to the pollution of subordinate leadership and followership. This pollution reveals itself in the form of timid leadership that can also be termed blind loyalty. Blind loyalty is when persons see wrong actions and attitudes and turn the other way as if they did not see it. They remain faithful to the perpetrators; to do otherwise may interfere with promotion or reward later.

What happens to the seekers of God's divine favor, presence, and provision when the one proclaiming such attributes exemplifies a life and leadership of fear rather than faith, timidity rather than tenacity, and heresy rather than holiness? I contend that many of the congregations with such leadership take on the tenor of that leadership. Everything does rise or fall on leadership. The overlooked result of this scenario is a perishing pew. The congregation loses confidence, respect, and trust in leadership. They will not say much nor voice their opinions. They will simply walk away, taking with them valuable talents, tithes, and time, or they will become stillborn. The perishing pew is looking for strong, bold, spirit-filled, God-envisioned leadership.

Timid, compromising phonies and fakes will only prolong the agony of spiritual pollutants. Covenant relationships are severed, proper stewardship is watered down, and authority is tampered. In all cases, those in the pew perish while the injured pastor moves to the next congregation under the guise that no one would work with him or her at the previous church.

3. The third key pollutant is <u>little or no ministry.</u>

One of the most telltale signs of the presence of spiritual pollutants is the presence of little or no ministry initiatives. When we compare the admonition of Scripture to the conduct of activities in churches, we cannot help but conclude that we are out of step with our mission. Many churches within our persuasion possess one-dimensional ministries, a failing Sunday school followed by a worship experience with preaching as the apex. Many of our parishioners leave the church just as they came, with little or no fulfillment. Although Sunday school and worship can be quite exciting and fulfilling, there must be concrete ministries that reach people at their points of need. What we preach and teach must present Jesus as practical. How we do church and ministry must also be practical and follow the model Jesus laid for us. The absence of relevant ministries is the paramount indication that the church is in a state of stagnation, and the absence of growth is certain. In the absence of ministry the church is not dead, but ill, polluted, and spiritually malnourished.

Ministry simply means service—services offered to meet the needs of the congregation and the community they serve. Jesus left a clear task for those who would join the cause of kingdom building. That task can be called a number of things. Any way you size it up, it boils down to ministry or service! The church must offer people something different from the dull daily routine found in most walks of life. The church must make every attempt to meet needs. What other purpose claims her reason for existence? Ministry also gives the church opportunity for financial growth and rewards. We will talk more about those opportunities under Part III: The Prescription.

We could go on and on about the pollutants present in many of our situations. The intent is to raise awareness of the demise happening in our churches today. At the foundation of this demise is what I have come to see as a poor understanding of stewardship. The principle of stewardship takes into account who we are, what we are, what we have, what we do with what we have, where we are going, and how we get there. Our time, talents, tithes, health, environment, and relationships speak to the principle of stewardship.

I am confident that this work will raise the necessary awareness so that this sleeping giant, the body of Jesus Christ, will live out the true meaning of its faith and will meet the mandates of our Lord.

What have you, as a leader, identified as the leading cause of detriment where you are? Can you give a proper diagnosis of the illness, if any, within the lives of your pews and pulpit? It is necessary that we concentrate on the cause and not the symptoms. Trying to solve symptoms is like placing bandages on cancer. Perhaps it is time to call for renewal. Begin with yourself. Don't be afraid to perform self-examination. It is the prerequisite to repentance! Call the body of Christ to a time of analysis. If what we are doing and where we are going is not theologically sound and scripturally intact, we need to redirect our efforts. Are we just going through the motion of ritual at the risk of resounding failure? Is every member where you are receiving what God intends for them through your witness?

I submit to you, my distinguished brother or sister, that the answers given will do nothing less than bring you to a place of responsible reflection or repetitious ruin. If you always do what you've always done, you will get more of what you have. Leading is not an easy task. I have found that most leaders give up in the hour of weariness. God has called you, man or woman of God, to a task of change. It must begin with you. Prayer with improved intimacy with God will help you stay focused. It is not an attitude of failure or giving up, but one of adjustments. Learn to adjust. Change is a constant. We cannot be the change, but we must adapt to the change. We must recognize that we are change agents and not the change. I know how painful and stressful it is to watch those who fight the change while you suffer from their ignorance. You must stand tall, Prophet. You must be teachable, Pew

Dweller. The end result is a thriving pew, and hence, a growing pew. The alternative is a perishing and polluted one. God bless you. You are not alone.

PART III
· · · · · · · ·

The Prescription

SIX

The Prerequisite of a Proper Stewardship

The very root cause of the church's dilemma is the lack of the proper stewardship principle. It is my intent to clearly define this principle prior to moving into the sections that suggest meaningful solutions to many of the ills that face us in our personal struggles with stewardship mandates and corporate and personal finances in the body of Christ.

The number one destroyer of a church is an improper understanding of stewardship. Everything we have (time, health, relationships, talents, property, the word of God, our bodies, the air we breathe, positions, finances, and existence itself) is given to us by God. The prerequisite to a proper stewardship focus is acknowledging that God owns everything (Ps. 24:1). Any misconception of this basic fact of existence points to the failures we now experience in various aspects of our lives. God has granted to you and me the awesome responsibility of managing the affairs of his estate, of managing everything he owns. God has equipped you and me with the necessary gifts, qualifications, and abilities to fulfill that responsibility.

To give a proper foundation for the understanding of stewardship, we must understand a covenant agreement. The foundation of this awesome concept is the fact that God has entered into "covenant relations" with man. It is here that we find a tremendous theme developing. A covenant is an agreement between two parties. The party of the first part pledges to abide by the terms of the covenant, while the party of the second part also agrees to abide by the terms of the covenant. In the ancient Hebrew custom, neither party could alter the conditions of the covenant. It was binding as an everlasting and eternal agreement. God has extended this ancient agreement with the church, believers, and his people: that he would remember his promises, he would make provisions, and he would give protections to his people as long as they abided by the covenant. He has entrusted them with the affairs of the agreement, which for this specific dispensational time remains valid.

Any person who transgresses the covenant is said to be a covenant breaker. Covenant breakers are individuals who habitually disobey the conditions of the covenant and only have limited protection, promise, and provision, if any of these conditions at all. While in this condition of limitation, they become content, complacent, and comfortable with a limited lifestyle in Christ, never really experiencing the fullness of his love and unlimited resources. They are said to always be in need of something, and they never rest in or rely on the peace and providence of God. Eventually they will become robbers of God, themselves, and others.

Covenant breakers also create for themselves a perpetual curse of lack, sickness, unsound mind, uncertain existence, and wandering direction. The implication from the word of God is that we should separate ourselves from these kinds of people. Pray for and encourage them, however. This may sound like foolishness to the secular mind; however, for those who vow to serve God as a believer, boundaries of action are present to guide our journey.

With this foundational understanding, let's now revisit the principles of stewardship.

Persons whom God has trusted with the responsibility of stewardship are called stewards. A steward must be careful to understand that management is not ownership. Stewardship is based primarily on what we do with what we have been entrusted with and secondarily with how much more of it we can produce. God has made each of us a steward and has equipped us with gifts and talents according to our abilities, enabling us to carry out the task of management. Christian stewards serve the Lord with thankfulness and appreciation because of God's trust and are concerned with how they will multiply what God has given them to benefit themselves and others, returning the faithfulness back to God, rather than with how much more they can get. Equally important is the fundamental providence that the stewards act on behalf of God, his purposes, and not their own.

Failure of a right stewardship principle is realized when the church does not follow it. For example, in any business arrangement, the mismanagement of the business's affairs will certainly lead to insolvency and lack. The business cannot operate apart from the purpose of its existence and survive. If God owns everything, and God has placed us as stewards over his estate to manage and prosper it, it stands to reason that we must operate within the parameters of his order, purpose, and will. Operating within a set of prescribed prerequisites that have proven to be failure proof is simply the smart thing to do. If God owns everything and has created everything without any counsel or input, then it also stands to reason that he knows what he is doing.

There are two reasons failure is realized: First, failure is realized for the most part when the manager decides that the owner knows less than he or she does and can do less with the resources than he or she can. Second, failure is realized when the manager covets ownership while still functioning in the manner of a steward, not recognizing he or she will never become the owner. Take a moment and think about this concept. We are not given the responsibility of creating the world or the church, but simply managing them. However, management brings with it the understanding that the manager must work to produce more of what he or she has responsibility over. Simply maintaining that to be managed is not enough. To misunderstand the fundamental principles of stewardship is an attempt at mere existence rather than living the fullness of life.

God declares that he knew us before we entered our mothers' wombs. The moment we cried and took our first breath, we became something awesome. Just imagine: a part of God is a part of what and who we are. At the moment of life, we start a wonderful journey that is totally owned by God. What we do with our lives is our choice, but a proper stewardship of our lives would compel us to seek the direction of the one who owns those lives. How we live gives God either glory or regret!

One of my favorite elements of stewardship is the stewardship of time, which speaks to what we do with the time we have. That in itself is an awesome theory. Every person is given twenty-four hours in a day. The time we have is only known by God. A meaningful time stewardship says that I must do all I can, while I can, every day that I can. I must use my time wisely and productively. Think about it. How much time do we spend trying to figure out how we are going to get to a desired place? How much time do we spend doing nothing? How much time do we spend setting goals? How much time do we spend in preparation to achieve those goals? How much time do we spend in prayer? How much time do we spend communing with God? Does the day just pass us by or do we account for every moment of that day?

God has promised each of us seventy years (Ps. 90:10). Where we end up and whatever state we end up in, pretty much, will be based upon what we did with the time and abilities we had. When we analyze this concept in our personal lives as well as our corporate lives, we cannot help but realize the failures that have taken place. It all relates to an improper stewardship. The blessings that the Lord has bestowed upon each of us are a testimony that God trusts us. When we fail to utilize all that we have to create more, to do more, to make God proud of how we manage what he has entrusted to us, we move into a posture of disorder. This disorder permeates every aspect of our lives in a negative way, so that we experience less, do the least, exploit others, and exploit the goodness of God. Life simply becomes mere existence without any fulfillment.

A right relationship with God, and functioning within that relationship, is the foundation that every other principle must stand upon. The opportunity to know the one who owns everything is a privilege and an obligation. What have we done with that opportunity? This speaks to another of my favorite stewardship principles, that of relationships. Scripture reveals that "eternal life begins at the point of knowing God and the Son" (John 17:3). God allows us to know him. He expects us to have intimacy with him. Reading the word of God brings us into an understanding of the mind of God. What God thinks, how he feels, his guidance and direction leading us to a place of fulfillment are contained in his word. What a blessed privilege it is to know the Lord. The fact that we were created means that we have little or no independent existence. Our beginning has its roots steeped deep in the thought that God willed our existence. Having an intimate relationship with that Creator is vital, and because of the dispensation of time we also must develop a sense of urgency to create that relationship.

As mentioned previously, there is little or no understanding of the concept of covenant relations by those either in the church or secular society. God has entered into an unconditional covenant and a conditional covenant with man. God gives us conditions of his relationship with man. He expects man to obey the principles and precepts of those conditions. Anyone who transgresses the conditions of the covenant is said to be a covenant breaker as a result of faithlessness.

We also face the burden of missed opportunities to share with each other in meaningful relationships. We have a commonality regardless of the color of our skin, creed, or national origin. That one race could ever postulate that humans are of different species based on the color of one's skin is nothing more than dumb ignorance. Several years ago I was watching a commentary on the religious aspects of white supremacy. In this program the leaders of the group were teaching their followers that people of African descent were of a totally different species than Caucasians. These were professing Christians who said they loved God, Jesus, and country. A misunderstanding of the stewardship of relationships is the real reason one ethnicity would assume that God has elevated them above all others. We have a brotherhood by virtue of our creation by one and the same Creator. More enjoins us than that which separates us! What a tremendous opportunity to meet other people who have come out of darkness into his marvelous light or to meet other human beings in general.

An old Negro spiritual, "What a Fellowship," resounds loudly: "O how sweet to walk in this pilgrim way." How we share life's experiences with one another lends either pride or shame to God for creating us. We are all witnesses to the poignant fact that we have been poor stewards of relationships over time. It is a grand thing to appreciate human life!

A further analysis of how we exalt one group over another, lend special privileges to one group over another, or justify our personal agenda and appetites suggests that we are all for those rights and fail to understand "human rights." When our focus is gay rights, women's rights, black rights, children's rights, and other rights of fragmented division rather than human rights, basic God-given human rights, the evidence is clear. Yet the "corrupt church," not the "true church," has exploited this human life concept to perpetuate its corrupt nature and motives. I wonder how many relationships we have destroyed because we did not understand the stewardship of relationships. This is the foundational fallacy that leads to perhaps the most distasteful dissension in the church, and life, which is discussed in the following paragraphs.

Finally, my favorite subject is the source of the greatest lack and struggle within the church, the stewardship of money. We will focus on this for the remainder of the chapter. Because of the fallacious perspective of our relationships with God and each other, selfish greed, financial destitution, and justified thievery present themselves in almost every situation within the church. Much of this attitude stems from indelibly etched, deep-seated roots of an internalized oppressed slavery mentality! Yes, believe it or not, much of this self-destruction and destruction of others in order that one may gain has as its root cause the internalized social stigma that was and continues to be imposed upon a particular people.

This systematic social evil began with our ancestors during slavery. Willie Lynch was a slave owner in the West Indies. In 1712 he was invited to the colony of Virginia on the James River to deliver a speech to teach his methods of controlling slaves. The word *lynch* is said to derive from his last name. (For further enlightenment go to www.willielynchstory.com.) The Willie Lynch theory was that if the slave master created mistrust between the slaves and divided them for one solid year this spirit or mindset of distrust would perpetuate itself forever. What began as a slave master's attempt at economic destitution, ethnic distrust among a group of people, is now implemented by people of the same ethnicity upon their own. Its manifestation is seen in the self-imposed annihilation of each other through the same means with which slave masters divided families: destroy their self-worth by imprisoning them socially, financially, and morally.

Let's look at how that wrong relationship or a misunderstanding of it has hurt the body of Christ financially. When we do not believe that God will supply all of our needs and give us the desires of our hearts (right desires), which for some is financial independence, then we set out on a course that will give us all we want by any means necessary, or so we think. According to evangelical scholars, two-thirds of Jesus' parables dealt with money. What is this thing that so many are willing to do evil and wicked things, even in the church, to acquire? Well, money is only a tool, not a God. It is a medium of exchange. It is a vehicle to acquire goods and services. The more of it we have, the more goods and services we are able to receive. It is interesting to note that 1 Timothy 6:10 admonishes us that "the love of money is the root of all evil" and not money itself. What one's intent is for the money they have and the perceived power that they feel comes with the acquisition of it will lead that person down the path of destruction, or it will move that person into the trenches of service to those around them while also helping themselves.

We must understand that stewardship allows us to know that there is enough sustenance to go around when promised by God. Money in circulation is God in action! Consider Matthew 6:24b, which illustrates the concept that money in circulation is God in action. Here Jesus declares that no man can serve two masters. "Ye cannot serve God and mammon [riches or hoarded money]." Our concept of money and what to do with it has been shaped by what I call false presentations and a clearly defined plan to allow some to have it and others not to. Poverty is not a given. Poverty is a plan as well as a choice, just as financial independence is a choice for some. Sometimes poverty is the choice of the majority population or the wealthy—they perpetuate it upon the poor—and sometime it is the choice of the victim. Did Jesus see the economic system of our day? Did God, through divine providence, plan for a few to be well-off financially and for others to be poor? Has God predestined the poor to be poor and the rich to be rich, or is it a matter of attitude, aptitude, and practice? With all that Jesus left the church to do, did he not know that it would take money, as well as prayer, to accomplish the task of kingdom building? Does the leadership of the Christian church know the answers to these questions? If so, does that leadership have a plan to keep the church in bondage and themselves in a posture of gain? I really would like to know the clearly defined intent! If the leadership does not know the answers to these questions then my question is, what is the basis of their qualification to lead this institution in the areas of the church's organization, administration, and financial solvency? In Jesus' day, as it is today, money was controlled by the wealthy and only available for the wealthy.

In America there are thirty secular companies that control the wealth and money. There are thirty companies that determine the Dow Jones Industrial Average. To say that these companies and their CEOs got there on their own through completely honest means and hard work only is simply untrue. Much of that wealth came through the exploitation of the poor and deliberately not sharing opportunities with others. Some stole ideas from others, poor yet ingenious, who lacked access to marketing, manufacturing, and money. This is in no form or fashion intended to suggest socialism, but to aid one's fellow man with opportunity. As you progress to the heights of success, reach back and help someone else. This is the American way.

Only about 10 to 20 percent of the American population makes $50,000 a year or more. Most people never take full advantage of the abundance and opportunities available due to a misdiagnosis of the tool of money and wealth and deliberate financial rape by gangsters of greed in leadership positions.

One last example: there was a time in America when some insurance companies had two different rate books when selling insurance. They presented a low-cost rate book providing more coverage for Caucasians and a high-cost rate book offering less coverage for African-

Americans. When I was born in 1953, my daddy could have invested in certain investment vehicles at a rate of an 11–13 percent return on his money. This information was deliberately withheld from him in an attempt to keep him and his family poor.

In the Christian realm, the principle of giving and receiving is different from that of the world. You give to receive in the Christian realm. Let me clarify this concept. As mentioned earlier, the book *The Seed of the Equivalent Benefit* illustrates how wealthy leaders such as the Mellons, DuPonts, and Gettys were all broke at some point in their lives. The book shared how they used the principles of seed planting and harvesting from Scripture to gain their wealth. They would fill their pockets with nickels, dimes, and quarters and would give it all away to those they met during the day. When they passed out a given amount of money unknown to them, they repeated an affirmation: "I claim my thirtyfold, sixtyfold, hundredfold return with good to all concerned." The key to reaping a harvest was that you had to believe in the amount you expected to receive back. I believed in that principle because these are some of the wealthiest people in the world, and they utilized biblical principles of finance to get there. I thought the book had a profound message because these were not pastors or preachers. These were secular men who understood utilizing a principle to prosper, unlike many who take all they can in order to receive, no matter who it hurts, in some cases. These are two different philosophies. As a tool money can accomplish much. As a weapon it can destroy much. It all depends on whose hands are using it.

Consider the following. In any church or body of Christ is a conglomerate of people. Some of those persons will consent by signature to borrow $25,000 to $30,000 to finance a car. Some of those persons will consent by signature to borrow $100,000 to $200,000 to finance a home over twenty to thirty years. If two people can consent to set aside $500 to $1,000 a month to borrow that small amount of money, why is it that a church full of people has fears of leveraging $500,000 to $1 million over the same period of time for expansion, ministry, and mission? What if fifty people in your church decided that they would leave $10,000 to the church at their death? What if fifty people started

61

an investment of $1,000 per year for ten years (a $500,000 principal), invested at compound interest in a market other than the bank? (In my twenty-two years of pastoring I have seen a very small minority of persons bring this idea to fruition for the church's posterity.) Far short of what could be done!

We have a tremendous resource and reservoir sitting in the pews every week. Remember now, any of these persons will help prosper a bank, an insurance company, a finance company, or a mortgage company for something now and for something they want. Further, how many in your church have left, in the form of bequest, a sum of money for the church at their deaths? How many have left anything to the church as a living trust or as beneficiary to an estate? Why is it that, for the most part, in the African American church people will leave the church in worse shape than they found it? I am now in my fifth pastoral assignment, and with the exception of two to maybe five persons, the Church did not suffer any financial loss because of the deaths of members in those churches. I don't know whether to cry or rejoice. What is this disease that invades the faith of our pioneering fathers' and mothers' posterity? A people who possessed a pioneering spirit to develop what they had been given responsibility over as opposed to people today, who have more but would rather be settlers on the land handed over to them. Again it is the ownership rather than management factor, the "what's in it for me" syndrome, and a clear misunderstanding of how money works and how it should work for us all. Further, people have a false sense of security that dictates "I must get all I can," only to leave it to probate lawyers or those who have no clue what to do with it to expand it for themselves or the kingdom's work.

As an investment and insurance salesman for some time, I saw firsthand how the selfishness factor operated. For example, a man with a wife and two or more children would have inadequate life insurance coverage of $5,000 to $10,000 to leave his family if he died, and he was quite comfortable that it was enough. He had never been told about the types of life insurance coverage available—in fact it was deliberately withheld from him. So agents would sell African-Americans expensive low-coverage insurance when a different plan that would have better insured the breadwinner could be had at the same price. Having never been taught the "human life value concept," many heads of households of the African-American persuasion, which make up the African-American church, were forced into poverty in a time of plenty and created the same perpetual plan of poverty for their families for generations to come. The point is that this mindset is prevalent today in those who lead many of the African-American churches.

Let's say for the sake of clarity that a breadwinner earns $20,000 a year. Over ten years that is earning power of $200,000. This is earning power over twenty years of $400,000; thirty years, $600,000. He or she will earn a lot of money in his or her lifetime. That means in the event of premature death you will have to have that much cash on hand or have a vehicle that will create an immediate estate to replace that income. For example, $200,000 invested at 10 percent interest per year will yield $20,000 per year. Depending upon the type of investment vehicle, this principal could continue to grow while yielding that 10 percent income per year!

How many of us have made that kind of preparation? How many of us even know of such a concept? Why hasn't the church made that a foundation of their teaching ministry? Did you know it is a biblical principle? The Scriptures teach us in 1 Timothy 5:8, "if any provide not for his own, and especially for those of his own house, he hath denied the faith, and is worse than an infidel." The word *infidel* means *unbeliever*, which was the worst thing to be in Timothy's day. This is a spiritual concept that manifests itself in the earthly realm. Did you know that most people have a spiritual problem and not a financial one? When that kind of understanding enters into the spirit realm to handle spiritual affairs or the affairs of God on every level as leaders in the church, it is no wonder that we have the lack in our homes, extended to our churches, further extended to our communities, extended even further to our city, county, state, and national existence. That is an example in the natural realm.

The point is, if leaders have the mindset that they have to get all they can for themselves and never take a stand to break the curse of this perpetual spiritual poverty within the body of Christ, particularly of the African-American persuasion, then we will continue to see churches close and folk defect. All other forms of stewardship and the proper understanding of the stewardship of money are necessary.

Consider another aspect of the stewardship of money, finance, and giving. A Christian will spend the kind of outlay in our previous example for personal and material desires but will not give to the church tithes and offerings as God has required. Once again, a person who cannot accept giving at least 10–15 percent of his or her income to God through the medium of the storehouse, the church, for the support of the ministry and outreach, has a relationship problem and not an economic one, a spiritually malnourished thought process. I have had the experience of helping persons with housing, electricity, food, and clothing after they lost all they had through mismanagement and other careless money handling. Some of these people sold drugs, and some received big accident settlements, some in the millions of dollars. These persons had not been taught the principles of finance or money, how to get it, budget it, invest it, or manage it. My experience as a pastor has also given me the firsthand observation that many of the people the church helped did not give to the church, while those who did give lacked an understanding to give as prescribed by the Scriptures. In every case, when I counseled these persons to try and teach them principles of what they professed, they only wanted to survive for that day, not for a lifetime. Again, those who do not necessarily subscribe to the Christian notion use these biblical principles to obtain abundance and wealth. They really do not trust God, yet God trusts them with complete earning power and grants the ability to have such power. The tithe defies human logic and understanding. It is a matter of trusting God enough to obey! This obedience yields in quantitative results the proportion of the individual's qualitative heart condition when giving. Tithing and giving of offerings is Christian!

When people feel that there is no reciprocal benefit of their giving, it places them in a posture of failed blessings, spiritually and tangibly. It is also a result of a poor mentality—they feel they have been victims of schemes and scandals all their life. So what makes the church any different? When this is coupled with the fact that some in church leadership are self-aggrandized gangsters, it does not help. Further, many of those same leaders will not tithe themselves but will admonish their flock to be obedient. At any rate, giving is not based on others' agendas but on obedience to God.

It is interesting that those in the church will obey the boss on the job, will follow to the letter the doctrines and rules of that said job, but willfully disobey the doctrines of the church. They will faithfully follow the tenets of other organizations they are affiliated with but choose to do as they please when it comes to the church. The church is an integral part of God's covenant relation with man. Jesus, the founder of the church, set conditions and principles for the "called out ones," the *ekklesia,* to follow to ensure good success in their journey. Each church has a mission and vision statement along with a polity that each member vows to follow. Most people do not know nor understand that polity, and if they do, they willfully shun that polity that ensures their success as a Christian. Not giving tithes and offerings is at the core of most people's chaos. If a financial crisis should arise, most will take care of that matter, and the church will go lacking; some of these same people will approach the church and ask for help. Once again, a lack of trust in God and the covenant dwellers' disobedience are always at the core of any financial dilemma, both in their personal finance and the church's.

The solution to this perpetual lack is a renewed intimacy with God, a greater understanding of covenant requirements, a rededicated commitment to the obedience of giving, and a love for the church and her posterity. How do we come to know and apply the principles of stewardship so we can eliminate lack? Let's use the marital institution as illustration. In a marriage are three basic essential causes that will fulfill or destroy it. They are intimacy, communication, and finance. These essential principles find their foundation in the church. If these principles do not exist as necessary ingredients in the church, then the church must clearly redefine the essential principles that will prosper her in the mandates of that essentialness. These same ingredients will destroy her if they are not properly distributed and used.

We must clearly define what and who we are, what we have, and what we are to do with what we have! Jesus relates one aspect of this principle in a parable, Matthew 25:15–30: And unto one he gave five talents, to another two, and to another one; to every man according to this several ability; and straightway took his journey. Then he that had received the five talents went and traded with the same, and made them other five talents. And likewise he that had received two, he also gained other two. But he that had received one went and digged in the earth, and hid his lord's money. After a long time the lord of those servants' cometh, and reconkeneth with them. And so he that had received five talents came and brought other five talents, saying Lord, thou deliveredst unto me five talents; behold I have gained beside them five talents more. His lord said unto him, Well done, thou good and faithful servant; thou has been faithful over a few things, I will make thee ruler over many things; enter thou into the joy of thy lord. He also that had received two talents came and said, Lord thou deliveredst unto me two talents; behold, I have gained two other talents beside them. His lord said unto him, Well done, good and faithful servant; thou hast been faithful over a few things, I will make thee ruler over many things; enter thou into the joy of thy lord. Then he which had received the one talent came and said Lord, I knew thee that thou art a hard man, reaping where thou hast not sown, and gathering where thou has not strewed. And I was afraid, and went and hid thy talent in the earth: lo, there thou has that is thine. His lord answered and said unto him, Thou wicked and slothful servant, thou knewest that I reap where I sowed not, and gather where I have not strewed. Thou oughtest therefore to have put my money to the exchangers, and then at my coming I should have received mine own with usury [interest]. Take therefore the talent from him, and give it unto him which hath ten talents. For unto every one that hath shall be given, and he shall have abundance: but from him that hath not shall be taken away even that which he hath. And cast ye the unprofitable servant into outer darkness: there shall be weeping and gnashing of teeth.

Here Jesus explains the distribution of talents to three different individuals. Two of them expanded or produced more with what they were given. They managed the property of someone else in a proficient manner. The third individual simply took what he was given and did nothing with it but looked out for himself. Notice that the first two were given responsibility over more because of their faithfulness to what they had been given and the production of more of it. The third one had that he had taken from him because of poor management decisions and failure to produce more with what he had. Management does not simply mean watching over the entrustment of goods or services. Management brings with it the responsibility of producing more from what we have been entrusted. Accountability measures our ability to be trusted with more. If one cannot manage the smaller matters of money stewardship, how can that same individual expect a greater management responsibility? The philosophy of "I'm poor and don't have much" has been a wrong philosophy. It has set a foundation of always needing while overlooking what one does have.

Think about it. God has given us the responsibility of utilizing our resources and getting the best use out of those resources for a specific purpose ... meeting the mission as well as our needs! Something is wrong when the majority of the funds are generated for "private inurement," leadership benefiting by raising funds through other than biblically mandated practices. It is a concept that brings about prosecution by the Internal Revenue Service for those in violation. In the secular world, those who engage in such criminal acts (yes, fraud) are prosecuted to the highest order. Yet in the church we say, "God will get them" and never blow the trumpet of truth on these acts of exploitation and greed. Should the children of light and grace subscribe to a lesser standard than the children of the law and disobedience?

The first step in healing is moving from denial to acknowledgment. Denial is glorified self-indulgent ignorance. Individuals know what ought to be done but are in denial that they are enlightened by this truth! Such clichés as "we've always done it that way" and "stop trying to change the church" or "they're just fighting the program" are always indications that denial is in the midst. Until we come to a personal solemn assembly of self-repentance, we can never get to the corporate repentance so desperately needed in the church.

This chapter's intent is to foster a proper understanding of our covenant relationship with God and each other and the practical manifestation of the principles of the stewardship of money. Its intent was also to create consciousness among the many leaders of the church who have used this noble institution for their own personal gain through exploitation and greed, unlawfully, and through not knowing any better. Further, the intent was to cause conviction among the many in the pew who set up kingdoms for themselves on Earth, with "goodly houses" and other material goods, but leave the church in a posture of struggle because of their stingy attitudes and practices, yet hoping and praying that God will heal their bodies, grant them financial blessings, or fulfill whatever personal needs they may have. The great institution of the church is equipped with provisions to enhance her prosperity if people are willing to abide by the covenant principles she possesses.

I do praise God that "great is his faithfulness," and it is not based upon ours but his divine prerogative. My brother and my sister, as a people we no longer have the luxury of crying "We are poor" or "we do not have the education" or "we do not have the means or wherewithal." No, no, we are not in Egypt any longer. Although some would prefer the benefits of having someone else to think for and provide for them, we must move beyond selfish mediocrity. This time is for strong, envisioned, and qualified leadership following the direction of God. This is a time for a people who have been without to receive what has been given to them, though not yet manifested and though exploited by those who know the truth but do not practice the truth. This is a time of exposure and expression, prosecution and progression, freedom with responsibility, and blessing with accountability. This is a time of reliance upon God and self-reliance upon our own resources given by God. In this era there is no need for any body of Christ to be destitute, destroyed, deterred, detained, nor delayed. Resources are in abundance. As Jesus has so relevantly put it, "the harvest is plenteous, but the laborers are few" (Matt. 9:37). I submit to you that relevant mission- and ministry-minded laborers are few.

The second step to healing is to commit to the biblical principles of finance and to insure that every pastor and church is equipped with the necessary financial management training that will project the church into the twenty-first century of prosperity. These principles of proper financial management for clergy and church can be taught through such great mediums as Chitwood and Chitwood, a tax and church accounting firm that helps the church and pastor develop the foundation of money management and pastoral care right with God and the IRS. You can find them online at ChitwoodandChitwood.com. They are located in Nashville, Tennessee, and are reputable and recommended. I would recommend that if you contract other accountants you obtain one who specializes in nonprofit taxation and law. It would also be a good idea to retain a good tax attorney that also specializes in nonprofit taxation and law. Also available are a number of church financial administration software packages. This will enable the serious pastor and church financial staff to keep accurate records and reports. Certain packages will also allow pastors and church secretaries to keep up with membership attendance, giving, tax statements, W-2s, 1099s, and other tax forms, as well as proper deductions for church employees. God gives the faith community the opportunity to prosper; therefore we, the members of that community, must be responsible for what God gifts to us and accountable for it as well.

SEVEN

Financing Relevant Mission and Ministry

One of the books that has influenced my position concerning the church and her mission through relevant ministries is *Economic Empowerment through the Church* by Dr. Gregory Reed. A tax accountant, attorney, and a member of the Internal Revenue Service Advisory Board, Dr. Reed has laid out, in simple terms, a methodology of financing the mission of the church by creating relevant ministries. Jesus gave us the mission, what we must do, in at least five commission verses: Matthew 28:19–20 (Go ye therefore, and teach all nations, baptizing them in the name of the Father, and of the Son, and of the Holy Ghost; Teaching them to observe all things whatsoever I have commanded you; and, lo, I am with you always, even unto the end of the world); Mark 16:15 (Go ye into all the world, and preach the gospel to every creature); Luke 24:46-48 (Thus it is written, and thus it behooved Christ to suffer, and to rise from the dead the third day: And that repentance and remission of sins should be preached in his name among all nations, beginning at Jerusalem. And ye are witnesses of these things); John 20:22-23 (And when he had said this, he breathed on them, and saith unto them, Receive ye the Holy Ghost: Whosoever sins ye remit they are remitted unto them; and whosesoever sins ye retain, they are retained); and Acts 1:8 (But ye shall receive power after that the Holy

Ghost is come upon you: and ye shall be witnesses unto me both in Jerusalem, and in all Judea, and in Samaria, and unto the uttermost part of the earth). Paul in his letter to the church at Ephesus, Chapter 4:11 (And he gave some apostles; and some prophets; and some evangelist; and some, pastors and teachers) tells us who will play major roles in accomplishing the mission. Much of the church's failure lies within the practical application of doing mission. The simplest form of doing the mission is ministry. The ultimate objective of the church is to lead as many as possible to hear the gospel message and to be confronted by Christ through the word of God and the example of our witness, hence receiving the gift of salvation, and to duplicate the process over and over again. Our product is Jesus, his gift of salvation, and our market is everybody. So how do we get our product to as many as we possibly can in the time frame granted to us by the divine providence of God? Through *ministry!*

The word *ministry* comes from several Greek root words. The one that fits our discussion is *diakonia,* which means service of religious and spiritual ministration and the work of a servant. This service is found and rendered in various forms of meeting the needs of people. Each person that has accepted the gift of salvation has been equipped with a specific function or gift that will enhance the growth and development of another person. Within a particular body of Christ are the ingredients necessary to enhance the mission of Christ through the ministry of persons in that body. Ministry involves investing in the holistic life of an individual. This holistic approach reaches into the spiritual, financial, physical, emotional, social, and educational realms of a person's life. Each person must experience growth in all of these areas in order to experience the fullness of life. Any area that is lacking will affect the other areas.

At the foundation of this existence, however, is the spiritual realm. A spiritual foundation is the fiber necessary to enhance all other areas of our journey. When investment is made within the body of Christ, in ministry, the mission of the church will be achieved. A clear understanding of our purpose will succeed our process. Unfortunately the church's definition and practice has been limited to a one-dimensional approach, in most instances, to accomplish the mission. Often what is missing is a clearly defined methodology or ministry model to get the mission task accomplished. It is the intent of this chapter to offer meaningful ministry models that have enhanced the growth and development of churches exemplifying a successful ministry model and to construct a practical, theoretical, and biblical model for the same. It is imperative that we do not lose sight of the holistic approach to this model. These three ministry models will address the spiritual, financial, educational, emotional, physical, and social venues of a person's life journey. It also must be understood that this involves more than money. Ministry invites and encourages people to live out their faith in joyful ways through the church.

The first model for financing the church for relevant ministries is found in the covenant philosophies of God to man and the desire to manifest that faith fact in one's own life and those of others. The principle of giving through the methodology of tithes and offerings is the faith fact revealed through practical means. When the discussion came up between Cain and Abel on why God found favor on Abel rather than Cain, God resolved the question by showing that Abel operated within the covenant relations he had with God, thereby offering to God the first and the best of all he had been given (Gen. 4:3-7). The tithe and offering is the practical revelation of one's belief in the covenant established between him or her and God, how one trusts God, and how God trusts them. It is more the quality of the covenant relationship than the quantity of that given.

Even the Internal Revenue Service acknowledges charitable giving and public offerings as the main source of the church's revenue. As a matter of fact any activity that renders itself in the form of profit-making ventures will jeopardize the tax-exempt status of that nonprofit organization if it is not within the operations of its incorporation, and a different filing status must be initiated. A church ministry or nonprofit must be organized by a set of prescribed principles and practical methodologies set forth by the authorizing agency (e.g., the state or the IRS). A separate filing form must be used when a nonprofit engages in profit-making activities (e.g., chicken dinner sales, fish dinner sales, bake sales, raffles). Furthermore, the IRS allows a 10 percent deduction for itemizing filers for their contributions.

Successful churches teach the principle of the tithe and offering coupled with faith in God to multiply that which he has promised. Your quest to have relevant ministries and finance them must begin with the tithe and offering covenant. It is a travesty and hypocrisy to ask people outside of your church body to support financially what those inside will not support! This principle must be understood before we can take the next step. If it is not understood, it speaks to the lack of clear understanding of the covenant relation between God and his creation and not the amount of money received in the offering. The tithe and offering is the foundation. The tithe and offering is the foundation. The tithe and offering is the foundation.

Every individual within the body of Christ should commit to contributing at least 15 percent of his or her income to the ministry of the church. Ten percent is the tithe, while 5 percent is for alms and other benevolent enterprises and offerings. If you understand this principle then you are in for a treat when you add the formula Jesus gave for the multiplication of that 15 percent. His formula for growth is a formula of multiplication, not addition. Let's say your congregation has one hundred members, and each member averages $10,000 in annual income. That's an income pool of $1 million. Fifteen percent of that pool is $150,000 in revenue to the church's ministry. Suppose those one hundred learn the principle of duplication as Jesus taught and each share the gospel message with one person, who each commit to contributing 15 percent of their annual income to the ministry of the church.

Now the multiplication factor increases exponentially when true ministry reaches those within and outside the church. For example, suppose you decide to invest enough money to start an adult and youth softball team. People in your surrounding area who are not members of the church become interested in that outreach initiative. You have the potential of eighteen additional persons joining the church. This growth principle began with the foundational principle of the tithe and offering. Can you imagine what the numbers would look like if you doubled everything? The key is to help someone. Invest in the sixfold holistic life of an individual. Teach them the gospel message as it was practically manifested in their own life. Teach them to give back what was given to help them. Teach them to duplicate the process all over again with someone else. Now you have a team of giving, saved, committed people who will duplicate their efforts. It is the most beautiful thing you ever wanted to see! The model must begin with this principle. In the day of our Lord, there were three modes of giving: the tithe, the offering, and the alms. It is interesting to note that 20 percent of a person's increase was given for alms or to help the needy.

Another factor regarding the tithe and offering is the principle of reciprocity. Reciprocity simply states that whatever you plant will return back to you. When you release obedience, the reward for obedience automatically returns. When you release faith relevant to the seed you plant, the system of reciprocity must return something back to you. When you make an investment in the stock market, you look for a return. Your return is based upon the type of investment vehicle and the state of the market. No matter what faith you have or what your expectation is, your return is based upon something you have no control over. You are at the mercy of market conditions. The rules of stock market investing set the conditions. God has set the rules as well as the market conditions relative to the tithe and offering. Your return is based on your obedience, faith, and seeds planted in service. As your congregation grows, your tithe on the gross amount of revenue received by the church opens a window of abundance that is beyond comprehension. Tithe in other relevant ministries that are also rendering service to humanity. What an exciting journey! Remember a previous principle: money in circulation is God in action.

The second model of financing relevant ministries within your church is an analysis of the needs within that church and those of the surrounding community, a theoretical approach, known as demographics. Careful inventory of those needs will present opportunities for ministry. Each ministry initiative encompasses growth potential. Most pastors and congregants do not realize the golden opportunity right across the street and one block over from where they worship every week. If the church is willing to extend her mission beyond the sanctuary, major sources of funding (discussed below) are available to aid that mission. The love concept principle dictates that we must create an environment for all of God's people to grow in every area of their lives. Society desires to see people productive. Once again this principle is rooted in the tenet of covenant relations.

As a former member and the only area pastor at that time of a three-county grassroots initiative during the Clinton-Gore administration, I was amazed at the amount of money waiting to be claimed by those who would do what the church has advocated since the beginning of her existence. Most black churches are situated within Empowerment Zones or Enterprise Communities—areas or communities that are blighted and need restoration. Effective coalitions between churches and other grassroots organizations would prove economically worthwhile. Hundreds of millions of dollars await you. (Heed caution, though, my brother and my sister. Be advised that if you embark upon this venture, you must not misappropriate nor mistake the fact that careful record keeping and application of funds are paramount!)

Isn't it a wonderful thing that now the church can enjoy the benefit of receiving funds for needed ministries that should have taken place within the community you serve anyway? (Note: I am willing to advise, instruct, or aid with the proper application of this venture. My contact information is on the back cover.)

Another source that warrants investigation is city government. Most philanthropists and grant makers, particularly the federal government, look for municipalities through which to fund initiatives. You in the church are taxpayers. Ask, seek, and knock! Don't be afraid to seek partnership with these entities without any fear of strings-attached funding. Note: Many of these funding sources will not advertise because they do not want you to know. You must also be aware of what is called *turf*. Those who are already participating with these funding sources will not invite other participants. If you do not know, you will not ask. Now you know.

Another area of funding sources is city government funds for housing. Funding is also possible through the state department of health and human services. Some municipalities that own their electric and utility firms charge late fees that result in CDBG (Community Development Block Grant) funds. Some of these funds are set aside for nonprofits. Millions of dollars are available for health initiatives. Awareness grants for educating your congregation on cancer, AIDS/ HIV, and other health concerns are available. Funds are made available through county health departments for health screening initiatives. Don't be misled; you have a right to participate in the "spoil." Do not be fooled by the smoke screen of "separation of church and state." You are both, the church and the state. You are a Christian and a citizen with rights.

One more interesting point is the pool of millions of dollars already at the disposal of the faith community. If you have one hundred churches operating within a given locale with an average annual revenue of $100,000 each, that's an operating pool of $10 million annually. Multiply that by ten years, and you have economic leveraging of $100 million! You think maybe some housing initiatives, economic development initiatives (restaurants, small businesses, clinics, schools, etcetera), child care development centers, senior citizen care, recording studios, and God knows what else could be realized with that kind of clout? Additional income potential is in abundance for those who are willing to collaborate. Guess who already knows about your potential and takes every advantage of it daily? Those who are already aware of your leveraging power are bankers, city executives, entrepreneurs, county and city governments, politicians, and oh yes, some clergy officials also.

I ask you: are we operating a den of thieves or a house of prayer? When we recognize that the despair, degradation, and destitution of an area are equal to the opportunity within that area, we are on our way to creating ministries that many more than a few are willing to support and fund. Are you a servant or one who desires to be served, my brother and my sister?

The third model of financing relevant ministries is available within your congregation. Consider the many products that each person within your congregation consumes each week, month, and year. What if there was a way for your members to buy from each other and have the proceeds fund ministries within the church? There is such an avenue, but most of our congregations are not aware of or exposed to it. Each week parishioners spend hundreds of dollars on goods and services. Other people profit from those dollars; why can't the church? Farfetched, you say. Well, many institutions of higher learning are capitalizing on the dollars spent by students and staff in the form of endowments for that institution. It is only within the African-American community that dollars touch hands once and then leave that community, whereas in most other communities dollars touch the hands within that community at least sixteen times before leaving that community. If each person within your congregation would leave at least $5,000 in an endowment bequest at their death, think of the possibilities of funding ministry. When Moses asked God what to do when faced by the barrier of the Red Sea and trailed by Pharaoh and his army, God simply asked, "Moses, what is that you have in your hand?" (Exodus 14:15–21)? What he needed to overcome his dilemma was right at his disposal. The luxury of excuses is moot when compared to the resources available to us. Perhaps we'd rather complain and murmur while leaving Egypt, or better yet, some would just rather stay there.

Churches all over America have embraced the challenge of changing communities, altering conditions, and enhancing relationships. These noble and courageous men and women of God have blazed paths that will secure the posterity of their churches for generations to come. Some years ago pastors in Detroit partnered to buy franchises within the community they served. Although they were of different denominations, they crossed those lines to institute ministry through economic and personal development. That's real church mission and ministry. Another renowned brother changed the face of the community of Harlem's housing conditions and catapulted the church he pastored into renewal and revival within and without the walls of the sanctuary. (Note: I am deliberately not mentioning the names of these great giants for fear of leaving some out, recognizing that there are so many who not only talk ministry but do ministry). Their success stories of housing for HIV/AIDS patients, clinics and hospitals for the underprivileged, and pre-kindergarten through twelfth grade schools under the auspices of church-related initiatives just excites me to no end.

What else should the church be involved in? This is the practical and theoretical gospel of our Lord Jesus Christ! When a denomination or church body boasts of 1 to 2 million members who raise millions of dollars annually, to the tune of $75 million to $85 million, yet rare instances of real ministry are recognizable all over the country, it is a travesty. Listen, the need is not financing; the need is not educated people with know-how; the need is to change the vision and focus of the leadership from themselves to God and the mission of his church. Perhaps the nature of leadership to lean away from these kinds of faith-based initiatives is due to an inability to incur the financial scrutiny. After all, we are the church; we do have financial means; we do have ministry models; and we have the know-how. What could the problem be?

This biblical model for financing relevant ministries is proven time and time again throughout the Word of God. It is contained within the theme of this sacred writ from Genesis to Revelation. It begins with the fact of God. He is the creator and maker of all things. God is the ultimate reality of existence. God is set apart from humans. He alone is self-existent, infinite, eternal, immense, and immutable. God has and does speak to man, and His word is ultimate truth. He is Lord over the entire universe and is in charge or rules all things for His benefit and glory. He is worthy of adoration and praise. God is love having shown this love in a proactive way through the incarnation and manifestation of our Lord Jesus Christ, and this love provides promises, protections and provisions for all, especially those who are His. Hebrews 11:6 (but without faith it is impossible to please him: for he that cometh to God must believe that he is and that he is a rewarder of them that diligently seek him), proves this resounding theme of the Bible that God desires to bless His people. This theme is a love story between a loving God and His people. God loves us and desires for us to reciprocate that love to our fellow man through ministry which is service. The point here is that God has provided all things necessary to carry out relevant service within our communities. Hindrances to this model are simply because the faith community is not aware of the model, do not believe the promises that undergird the model, or refuse to participate in the model for ministry.

EIGHT

Revitalizing and Empowering the Husbandman

Lest it be too late, there is a real need to reestablish the position of pastor in all of its integrity. A few years ago, scandal invaded the horizon of pastoral leadership in this country. There was one attack after another against pastors and one ministry demise after another. The lingering repercussions of those scandals were that every preacher, pastor, minister, and ministry came under serious indictment and became suspect to the world and legalistic Christendom. Although there has been much reconciliation and restoration, there still lies in the back of the minds of some that ever-present question about the integrity of the preacher. There is some justification for this perspective, however, because some of our distinguished colleagues are still practicing the art of impropriety. We've touched on that issue in a previous chapter. At any rate, a revitalization of the office of the husbandman is needed.

This term *husbandman* is both male and female in essence. It is a term that references one in charge of a specific task or function. At one time it referred to the first recipient of the increase realized from the husbandman's labor. The divine prerogative of God has established the church as the dispensation operative in God's scheme of time. Contextually, the church has as her overseer the office of pastor or husbandman. Within any context of Christendom, the pastor or husbandman is the first partaker of the fruits experienced from the labor of that husbandman. It is not one of those philosophical equations that can be dissected by mere logic but exists under the shadow of the divine prerogative. The word *husbandman* comes from an agricultural term, signifying a laborer: one who plants, waters, and nurtures a particular crop. A deeper meaning of this profound tiller is one who digs the land for cultivation. An amateur may see only an empty field of grass, shrubs, and still land. However, to the husbandman what lies beneath the uncultivated soil matters. The husbandman simply works at making something out of mere dirt by plowing and tilling, plowing and tilling, and plowing and tilling until the land is ready for seed. The husbandman knows that the land must be prepared to receive seed. Every other individual may feel that the labor of the husbandman is futile, since no one else has been able to produce anything on the same land. But to the true husbandman resources are in abundance where nothing seems possible.

I can remember many, many occasions during the summer months when my brother and I would boast about what relatives we would stay with. I would stay with our grandfather and grandmother, and he would stay with our uncle. My grandfather is the reference for me that best described this noble call of the husbandman. Every morning he would rise around 4:00 AM. First he would pray, and then he would head for the back porch. I followed in earnest inquiry as to what in the world he could see or do at 4:00 AM. He would peruse the morning sky to see what signs had formed for the day's weather forecast. With no degree, no meteorological training, this man of God would tell me if it were necessary to prepare the mule or prepare for inside work for the day. He would work at tilling the land, caring for livestock, nurturing the same as if it were his personal creation. His love for nature and that which God had created out of nothing was special to him and all husbandmen.

I watched as he meticulously plowed and plowed some more, then planted and planted some more, with archaic tools of craft. He even handed the plow over to me from time to time so I could get the feel of having the awesome authority of cultivating that owned by God. He wanted me to experience this fundamental way of life without luxury. It is an interesting yet simple principle: if you are ever taught the basic fundamentals of living, when luxury escapes you or the basics of life are torn away, you have the tools of know-how to survive. This was his duty, his responsibility to his master, to take that given him and honor God by producing something more out of it. Yes, it is basic, it is fundamental, it is noble, and it is right for the husbandmen to be first partaker of the fruits. That harvested from the labor of the husbandman, and the grace of God, should be enjoyed by the laborer of the harvest.

So then how does this agricultural concept bear on the notion of revitalizing and empowering the husbandman, the pastor? The call to pastor is one nobler than any other profession in existence. The profession that is the most thankless, the loneliest, ever stressful, in constant demand, underpaid, overworked, beat up, beat on, picked on, and unappreciated, yet the most rewarding, caring, loving, dependable, responsible, accountable, ever present, enabling worker and the most faithful I know is the noble profession of pastor/husbandman. Those called of God for this office are truly a special breed. Often I ask myself not only how do we keep going but many times why. Why does this servant of God seem resolved to take the abuse of ungrateful, sometimes mean and vicious people? What is equally amazing is that many of these willing vessels have more than one vocation, while others have experience and expertise (in the secular realm) in areas that would certainly offer greater monetary rewards, yet they remain faithful.

This really is where the agricultural concept of husbandman-ship bears relevance to the pastorate and its revitalization. The pastor has no idea what lies beneath or within the heart/soil of an individual. He or she is dependent upon the spiritual nature of a person, the holy order intent of God within the context of his creation. Somehow God places within the spirit of the pastor/husbandman a knowledge of what ought to be concerning God's creation. It is often called VISION! Vision is bringing about a desired result from a situation. Vision is seeing what can be and bringing that thing to fruition. While mission tells what must be done, vision promotes the methodology of how it is to be accomplished. Pastors, who are the husbandmen, are visionaries, cultivators, developers, and architects of God's creation. They have the awesome responsibility of developing the leadership within them and around them. They are responsible for creating, producing, and developing something out of the unrealized something handed them by God. Regardless of how the responsibility came about, ultimately God holds the pastor accountable.

You ask, why hold these persons accountable? Well again it is the holy order or divine prerogative of God. This profession is the only one I am aware of that is held accountable for other persons' actions, one that must give account of the conduct of others. Other professions hold individuals accountable for personal conduct and practice. Only the pastor is held accountable for the personal conduct and practice of those placed under his or her authority. No other entity, whether it is bishop, superintendent, lay officer, president, politician, or any other, has the right, privilege, or authority to interfere with the responsibility or authority of the pastor. Nothing or no one should in any way, form, or fashion, either implied or explicit in appearance, usurp the authority of the pastor. It is not only dangerous but unethical, immoral, anti-God, and certainly unprofessional. Again, I am speaking of the "called of God" pastor. The honor of this call has been discussed in Chapter Four, so we won't repeat the importance of the call. However, we will reiterate that this principle of revitalization of this office is intended for "the called pastor."

Why revitalization and how do we do it? Prophetic theologians and scholars of evangelical and dispensational persuasion believe that we are at or near the end of the church age or the period of grace. This period began at Pentecost and will end with the Rapture. Their belief is that the church is the institution ordained by God to receive members; instruct, discipline, and develop believers; create ministries; and evangelize the world. At the head of this institution or the church is Christ, and the administrator of the task of the church is the pastor. When other positions within the church replace the office of pastor, where does the leadership come from to guide the work of the church? Many pastors have been reduced to doing nothing more than overseeing church work, the administrative rather than the mission-oriented work of the Church. Church work is okay, but it does not ensure growth, spiritual or personal. Church work does not ensure ministry; it only ensures that church work is done. Church work is merely that, church work, and not the work of the church. Church work is internal business and that is okay, but it does not have the "good success" that goes along with the work of the church. The pastor must keep the congregation focused on the work of God, the work of the church. The pastor must scan the horizon of God's intent and prepare the saints of God for the work of the church.

When the pastor is reduced to only getting a salary, showing up on Sunday and at midweek Bible study, admittedly that is good, but while the church doors are closed most of the week, the body is out of divine order, and the office of pastor is reduced to that of a hireling. When someone or something other than God, or the mandate of the christological Logos, dictates the duty or function of the pastor, the office is reduced to that of a hireling. So revitalizing the pastor simply places the office and the body back into right order. The body is blessed, and the pastor is blessed, for operating within the realm of the gift and God's purpose. Now there are some who will cry aloud that there were many churches that were laity led. They were laity led, yes, but not pastored.

As emphasized previously, the biblical context of pastoring is illustrated by a shepherd leading, tending, and feeding a flock of sheep within a sheepfold. The shepherd would lie in the opening or gate of the sheepfold to keep sheep in and predators out. He was equipped with a staff and a rod. The staff was long and curved at the end to hook straying sheep around the neck to bring them back into the sheepfold. The rod was almost in the shape of a bat, prepared especially for that particular shepherd to ward off predators. Sheep are not going to protect sheep. A shepherd will. Sheep will lead other sheep to destruction, but a shepherd will lead them to destiny. So pastors are especially equipped shepherds given the task of watching over a particular flock. In tending sheep, shepherds are aware of the fact that the body of a sheep is so delicate that when they fall you must be particular in how you lift them, for the gases within their body will implode if not handled correctly, thus destroying a valuable piece of property. So pastors must be equipped in "soul care." For when one of his or her flock should stumble and fall, you must be careful how you lift them. The state of their soul is vulnerable, and they must be handled carefully. Any mishandling of their delicate soul nature could destroy them. Only trained shepherds knew how to handle the sheep. So it is with deliberate constitution that I reiterate: There must be a revival of the pastor. Any church, body of Christ, bride of Christ, whatever you term it that is without a pastor/shepherd (called, anointed, and sent by God) is merely a socialized gathering place going through the motions of church without the "candlestick" or the "angel."

So to every bishop over pastors, to every supervisor/presiding elder/superintendent in a supervisory capacity over pastors, to every pastor in contact with another pastor, and to every layperson under the care of a pastor, be careful how you treat that gift. Be careful how you treat those who have the awesome and divine command of watching over another's soul. That's an ordination instituted by God and not man, and what God has joined together let not man put asunder! While others are searching for what to do in the body of Christ, the pastor is equipped from his or her spiritual birth call with the knowledge of his or her duty. Any impediment against that call will be destructive to the body. I cannot emphasize this fact enough. The Scriptures are clear in John 10:4–5: and when he putteth forth his own sheep, he goeth before them, and the sheep follow him for they know his voice. And a stranger they will not follow, but will flee from him; for they know not the voice of strangers. When sheep are accustomed to a certain voice giving instruction and guidance, another voice will lend confusion so that the sheep may not know whose instruction to follow. However, when the sheep hear the voice of the true shepherd of their flock, they will not follow a strange voice. Within the context of this persuasion, serious thought and investigation ought to be the order of the day regarding the interference of other leaders dressed as pastors before the flock of the true pastor. The pastor with the appointment should be the only voice of instruction and direction the sheep hear within the right context of Christendom and churchmanship!

Finally, holding an office given by God in high esteem is setting oneself in a posture of reward, great reward. To give a pastor a drink of water is honor. To help him or her with the divestment of the robe is honorable. To assist the man or woman of God is like assisting God himself. What would God render unto his servant for service rendered unto him? It is such a great reward to serve the man or woman of God in any capacity. The quantity is irrelevant, but the quality of the heart condition is priceless! Try God and see what will happen if you talk the pastor up and not down. See what will happen if you cooperate and obey the vision of the pastor rather than analyze and attempt to kill it. Pray every day for your shepherd along with practical evidence of that prayer and see what God will do on your behalf. Honoring the covenant relations God has entered into with you and me is the most significant premise.

The fact that he loves us so much, that he would appoint pastors to watch out for and care for the welfare of our souls, is evidence enough that we should honor and take care of that gift. The heart of a pastor is what makes the relevance of the pastoral call so significant. A heart that is tuned into God's answer to the prayers of those pastored is a special anointing of God on the man or woman of God. A heart that focuses on how he or she can bring those God has given them responsibility over, to the place of seeing themselves as God sees them. A heart that is driven with passionate determination and spiritual fervor to inspire the people of God to walk in the success of God's mandated will. A heart filled with humility so that he or she will often receive hurt and the brunt of individuals' rage rather than perpetuate that hurt on his or her sheep. A heart that flows with the joy of filling others with the joy of the Lord is the true shepherd. What a noble and honorable vocation! What a noble and honorable individual! My Lord, bless your menservants and women servants everywhere. Restore the integrity and character of their call! In the name of Jesus!

AMEN

NINE

Economic Development, Empowerment, and Jesus

Does the Bible speak of economic development and personal empowerment as we know it? Why do we have poverty and lack in our society? Do you believe poverty is planned, whether by the poor or by oppressors?

Scripture tells us "the love of money is the root of all evil" (1 Tim. 6:10). I would like to add that the lack of it could possibly be right up there with the love of it. I propose that the lack of economic development and empowerment within our communities is the second greatest contributor to the blighted conditions, crime, and disease within those communities and a psychological condition that often fuels a desire to merely exist. It is second only to the greatest contributor, that of systemic evil and instigated poverty. Could it be that even church leaders have contributed to this deluge of missed opportunity due to a failure to know and investigate as well as an exploitation of realized resources unbeknownst to the source of the resources?

This chapter will continue to lend practical principles that when applied will be the center of solutions to the dilemmas cited above. Jesus tells us in John 10:10, "I have come to give life and give it more abundantly." We will identify what that abundance is and how it can and must be applied in the church.

One of the sound principles of economics is that one can only provide for others when he or she has the resources to do so. We have been misled by a few misnomers within the biblical context:

1. We have been taught to just go through whatever trials and tribulations we must and when we get to heaven everything will be all right.

2. People in general and black people in particular were cursed with color and poverty.

3. The church should only be concerned with getting people saved.

4. Pay your dues, do your time, and if you're fortunate you may be elected to a higher office or pulpit that brings financial reward. In the meantime stay where you are and don't be ambitious.

5. This is probably the greatest untruth: because Jesus was depicted as a poor carpenter from Nazareth the Christian shouldn't seek financial independence.

Quite the contrary is true. Allow me to stage an argument of evidence here. The word of God states that when they came into the house they saw the young child with Mary, his mother, and fell down, and worshiped him; and when they had opened their treasures, they presented unto him gifts: gold, and frankincense, and myrrh (Matt. 2:11). When you scrutinize the etymology of each of these three gifts, some wonderful knowledge unfolds. First of all, each of these gifts was a commodity of tremendous value. Gold has a twofold meaning: Gold was valuable as a coin commodity. It is said that the gold brought to Jesus by the magi would be valued in the hundreds of millions of dollars in today's American currency. This was enough financial means, in that day, to sustain him and his community of servants for his entire journey on Earth.

This is an interesting and marvelous illumination of a point that is significant to the rest of this chapter. Consider this point carefully and openly. Gold, metaphorically, speaks of sound doctrine and its effects; of righteousness of life and conduct. Myrrh is a gum resin from a shrubby tree that grows in Yemen and neighboring regions of Africa. The fruit is smooth and somewhat larger than a pea. The color of myrrh varies from pale reddish yellow to reddish brown or red. The taste is bitter and the substance astringent, and it acts as an antiseptic and a stimulant. It was also used as a perfume. It was one of the ingredients of the holy anointing oil for the priests, and it was also used for the purification of women. Myrrh was also used for embalming as an anodyne. Myrrh was a commodity of great demand and value in Jesus' day. Frankincense is a vegetable resin, bitter and glittering, and is obtained by incisions in the bark of the *arbor thuris*, the incense tree, and imported through Arabia. It was used for fumigation at sacrifices or for perfume. This too was another commodity of great demand and value in the days of Jesus.

So to sum it up, the gifts given to our Lord were all gifts that brought him great wealth while here on Earth. How would Jesus sustain himself and the disciples who would leave their livelihoods, sustenance, and ways of life to follow him? Was this simply a walk of faith, dependent upon what people would give them? Was this a group of religious fanatics who were hoping for someone to come along and free them from the bondage of manual labor? Did these men of God totally rely upon Jesus to provide for them what they had provided for themselves all these years? I believe, according to the divine enabling, that God endowed Jesus with earthly (material) substance and sustenance to provide for him and those who would commit to follow him to build the kingdom, just as he continues to do for those who truly love him and follow his will. What does that have to do with our subject matter to be discussed in this chapter?

I have never believed in the extreme teaching (call it and hall it, name it and claim it) of prosperity theology, although I do believe in prosperity. I also believe in divine providence. When God ordains a person or persons to obey a command from him, he also provides the means by which that command is carried out successfully. Once again, Jesus was to come to the world as any normal human baby, through the same human process. A woman, a virgin, would give birth without the aid of the seed of a man. His arrival is providentially encompassed in the Father's will. He did not come with all of his attributes, for he emptied himself, a doctrine known as kenosis. Therefore his Father, knowing what he would encounter on his earthly journey, prepared him with "earthly" sustenance. In order to recruit as disciples some who had good jobs, positions, and wealth, Jesus had to be prepared to offer them something in return to replace what they gave up. Sure, the promise of kingdom dwelling now and eternally was the greatest reward, but something else was needed to maintain the stamina and stability that went along with kingdom building. They still had to eat, sleep, and buy goods and services. They still had to pay taxes. Although the Scriptures are clear that Jesus did perform many mighty miracles for feeding thousands and caused a fish to cough up a coin fit to pay the tax demanded, such miracles did not occur all the time. They still had to take care of their families, just as you and I, in our day, must have some consistent sustenance to provide what we need if not what we want.

This is another significant point that church leaders and layfolk misunderstand or do not accept. Incorporated within this notion of kingdom building on Earth is development. There are six areas of development a person must experience for a successful life journey. These necessary life experiences in the social, educational, physical, financial, mental, and spiritual areas must be realized for a person to grow and develop as God would have them do.

At the core foundation of these areas is the development of the spiritual. It is the lifeblood of the existence of all the others. All the other areas of development are an extension of the spiritual. They are the backbone of existence, but the spiritual is the lifeblood. Spiritual development is the "empowerment factor" every human being must encounter prior to the sustained good success of any of the other areas of development. Herein lies the answer to our quest to identify the abundance that Jesus talks about in John 10:10. Consider this verse for a moment: The thief cometh not, but for to steal, and to kill, and to destroy: I am come that they might have life, and that they might have it more abundantly. I have come to give *life* and to give it more *abundantly*!

Life as defined from the biblical perspective is an interesting point. When God breathed into the nostrils of man the breath of life, *spirit,* then man became a living soul, *nephesh* in Hebrew. The context of this soul principle really means *life.* Encompassed in the soul are all the areas of life in which we need to develop. The very existence of an individual is centered on the development of the soul: our desires, our will, and our emotions. Destroy the soul, the life, of an individual, and you have a mummy, a person who walks around dead. These persons are dead to opportunity, dead to abundance, dead to the awesome talent and ability within them, and dead to the total fulfillment of life. When Jesus declared he had come to give life and give it more abundantly, he was saying that all of life's fulfillment, development, joys, successes, and abundance are accomplished in his sacrificial atonement for the soul, life, of a person. This is the saving of their soul.

Jesus inspires, encourages, and requires the development of the whole person through the salvific benefit, the transforming power of Jesus' atonement on the cross. That's abundances realized beginning. Only when the whole person is developed can he or she realize the potential within. Motivational speakers arouse only a part of that psyche. As good of a job as they do, it takes more than a motivational session to develop the whole person. The church of the living God, the true vine of the BODY OF CHRIST, is where this living water is supposed to be realized and distributed in its holistic essence.

Consider John 15:2–8, in which Jesus declares that fruit bearing is not enough (Every branch in me that beareth not fruit he taketh away; and every branch that beareth fruit, he purgeth it, that it may bring forth more fruit. Now ye are clean through the word which I have spoken unto you. Abide in me, and I in you. As the branch cannot bear fruit of itself, except it abide in the vine; no more can ye except ye abide in me. I am the vine, ye are the branches: He that abideth in me, and I in him, the same bringeth forth much fruit: for without me ye can do nothing. If a man abide not in me, he is cast forth as a branch, and is withered; and men gather them, and cast them into the fire, and they are burned. If ye abide in me, and my words abide in you, ye shall ask what ye will, and it shall be done unto you. Herein is my Father glorified, that ye bear much fruit; so shall ye be my disciples). More fruit bearing is not enough. Only when persons reach the "much" fruit bearing development stage are they really true disciples and possess the development necessary for abundant living. Fruit here means work and a work ethic, creativity, innovation, productivity, and ingenuity within a life. The financial, social, educational, mental, and physical success of an individual is tied intrinsically to the soul. The church must address the whole person rather than a one-dimensional aspect of that person. Much of what we do is address the symptoms rather than the cause of a person's lack of a fulfilled life. It was at the church that people encouraged political involvement, social involvement, educational achievement, mental ascent (the art of thinking), and financial success. The church must once again return to the principle of tending to the whole person, teaching individuals how to search the soul for the ideas God has planted there. We must teach individuals how to tap into the reservoir of ideas and unfulfilled realities within them that have created millionaires, multimillionaires, and billionaires.

When you consider an organization in the business of soul development that reaches a financial milestone of $90 million to $100 million per year, yet that development is secondary to personal financial gain, something is intrinsically wrong! The concept of soul development reached the pinnacle of its importance in the work of such notables as Dr. Martin Luther King Jr. and Gandhi. Their plight was to lift (develop) the downtrodden and the voiceless. What was so interesting about their methodology was not making people feel good about who they were but about a cause and their places in it. Soul development has a lasting effect on all its environs (only what you do for Christ will last). A great number of people, specifically African-Americans, have developed into financial giants, financially secure freedom recipients, and business owners and developers because of the foundational soul principle laid prior. The church and her leaders must realize that resources are not to be exploited but developed and multiplied. Exploitation of those resources is destructive to the soul of an individual, which will essentially be destructive to a neighborhood, a community, a nation, and a world. Destroy that essence and you destroy the person and the creative ideal quality of that person, hence shutting down the perpetual abundance principle.

Abundance was never only for the few and the elite. As a matter of fact the only reason it exists that way is because of those whose tactics are to destroy and exploit rather than to develop. They do not have the art of development or empowerment, except for themselves, for their perspective is to get all they can from those who have it while destroying the soul value principle. As I worked many years in network marketing, this principle was confirmed within me. The concept was if you help enough people achieve their dreams you can achieve yours. It was about people helping people with a common goal.

By utilizing the Nehemiah model, I want to share with you some interesting principles that provide a foundation for community, economic, and personal development and growth, which is God's intent. The Nehemiah model (from the Book of Nehemiah) is used to show what can happen when one individual has desire, dedication, determination, deliberation, declamation, delegation, and demonstration. This model contains a divine purpose agenda. I want to share with you what I call the four principles of the Nehemiah model.

The first principle of the Nehemiah model is finding God's purpose or will and submitting your personal will to his (Neh. 1). Nehemiah had a desire to see destruction, ruin, hopelessness, and despair turned into hope, renewal, revival, and construction. He had a desire to see his community and home and his people's lives rebuilt! His desire stirred his faith in God to call on the God who planted the desire in his heart; God desires that none should perish. This text is one of many, but it is probably the best to indicate the principle of the divine's intent of economic, community, and personal development. As the cupbearer of the king of Persia and governor of Jerusalem, Nehemiah's dedication was evident (Neh. 2) as he asked Artaxerxes I Longimanus (464–424 BC) for permission to leave his post of prominence and importance to dedicate his time to rebuilding Jerusalem. It was Artaxerxes I Longimanus (known as "long-handed") who stopped the rebuilding of Jerusalem, but later he changed his mind and authorized Ezra to lead many of the Israelites back from captivity to Jerusalem.

Nehemiah, knowing the risk involved, still pursued the king's permission to rebuild his hometown. He showed the character of determination, deliberation, and declamation (Neh. 2) when he encouraged the people to rebuild the walls. Even in the face of adversity and enemies, he accepted the challenge and called his people to stand! He went by night to survey the ruin from all sides while calculating the cost and the manpower to get the job done.

The second principle of the Nehemiah model is to clearly define the vision. Is there a cause, and is it of God? As it was then, there is still a cause for human and economic development. Make the cause known and the vision clear. The prophecy of Habakkuk 2:2 tells us, write the vision and make it plain upon the tables that he may run that readeth it. There can be no reservations, hesitations, or fear to accomplish the things of God. You must stay focused, focused my friend, focused! People who lose their dedication to God have lost sight of the prize. In losing sight one becomes selfish and introverted, attendant to one's own desires. Hope in the people whom you have been sent to build up and develop becomes lost in the maze of attention to their humanity and their lack of service and desire rather than engaging their divinity. People are frail and fickle at the same time. We all have human shortcomings, and we all pay more attention to those shortcomings as the basis of what a person can or cannot do. On the other hand, there is a divine side of every human being, a part of God in him or her, and when that spirit man is stirred and steered toward what he or she can accomplish as opposed to what he or she has not; when the soul of man is driven to what he has, rather than what he does not have; when this innovative energy of being suddenly realizes that it's more important to focus on what you can be than what you have been, something exciting and renewed is birthed.

When the real focus now centers on humanity and all of its weaknesses, we can slip into intent of greed and not the need. Therefore the "itis" diseases take hold: excuse-itis, position-itis, and title-itis. These three diseases are the premier sicknesses that hinder the development of vision. It's not easy focusing on a cause that those in need of it are not focused on when they fight against you, the visionary. You become the visionary, motivator, development manager, accountant, book-keeper, evaluator, facilitator, and everything else, it seems.

Prior to sharing the third principle of the Nehemiah model with you, I am reminded of a story I read about a man instructed by God to push against a very large rock. He eventually became obsessed with why he was not able to move the rock. Day after day he pushed and pushed, but the rock would not budge. Frustration began to set in, and one day he decided to ask God why he would not give him strength to move the rock. God replied, "I did not tell you to move it, just push against it." Sometime leaders lose sight of what their real purpose is. *Stay focused*!

Chapter 3 of Nehemiah gives us our third principle of the Nehemiah model: find and enlist others who are dedicated to the cause. So many times leaders deal with paid for leadership and followership and people who are not motivated. I learned a profound insight some time ago from a great leader and visionary, Art Williams, the founder of the successful and legendary A.L. Williams sales and marketing organization: "what they have done, they will do; what they have been, they will be." This simply means that there are people who want what you want and in turn what God wants. Find them, and develop them into your frontline leaders. Know the qualities of your people and use their gifts to aid in the development process. Be aware also that there are those who will continue to be what they have always been and do what they have always done. Let all the other negative stuff go. *Just let it go*! Surround yourself with like-thinking people—not robots or "yes" people, but other comrades with a cause. At least have these persons as your leadership team. Choose them, love them, encourage them, engage them, build trust with them, then develop them, then give them task to perform. That's delegation. Yes, delegate responsibility and share the cause. You can do more with these cause soldiers than by yourself. I must say here that you must spend time with those frontline soldiers. Become a family. At every possible point share the vision, reemphasize the cause! Finally, my brothers and sisters, there must be demonstration.

The final principle of the Nehemiah model is "get it done." Just do it! Nehemiah followed these principles and in fifty-two days the wall was finished. That's less than two months! Can you imagine? What could have taken years, months even, took just fifty-two days! Can you imagine what 1.5 million people could do with a focused and unselfish leadership? Can you imagine what 1 to 2 million could do if they had "minds to work"? Imagine what 1 to 2 million could do if they did not feel violated and exploited by leaders but were developed by leaders for the cause. Nehemiah does not give the number of people working on rebuilding Jerusalem; however, Chapter 3 does indicate it was nowhere near 1.5 million. What if 1.5 million people were focused on church development, community development, economic development, and personal development of their people? What if conferences, districts, and church leaders were focused on senior citizen housing, long-term nursing care, child care, jobs, health care, housing, and business ownership for her people? You know what? Those in your congregation are affected by all of this. They are either a recipient or a victim. Is there still a cause? There is.

Many where you serve have lost hope because they were sold a bag of goods that did them no good. Many within our congregations have set their dreams on the back burners because they can't dream anymore. In other words, we are living in a perilous time, with all of its star players, but times like these bring out the real people—those who see blighted conditions and quickly pronounce that we've got these conditions right where we want them. The churches I have pastored (St. Andrew in Wilmington, North Carolina, and St. John in Wilson, North Carolina) part of my past twenty-two years inspired me to move from a place of maintenance to one of ministry, from one of praying for people to go to heaven to helping them experience heaven right here. The visions were planted into my heart and we began (in Wilson, North Carolina) the Smith Street Project: From Stumbling Blocks to Stepping Stones. Our vision was to take the entire block of Smith and Church Streets for development. It was a fivefold vision initiative: a twenty-four-hour child development center, economic development, an after-school tutorial, HIV/AIDs and other health awareness initiatives, and housing.

The current statistics about the baby boomers becoming seniors create a need for assisted living and special health concerns that we now are not prepared to deal with. The lack of funding for mental institutions that frequently release borderline patients creates another opportunity for development to handle those needs. The release of prisoners who have served their time and will need some form of services to rehabilitate them back into society gives other possible development opportunities. Still other blighted conditions within a number of communities is clear evidence that a need and a cause exist. I believe the church is in an excellent position to provide services to meet some of those needs and at the same time achieve multiple kinds of development.

Economic development, community development, personal development, and empowerment are not questions of whether they are necessary or ordained by God. They are questions of when we will start focusing on getting the job done. There must be a clearly defined implementation of vision and execution from the leadership of the church that focuses on relevant methodologies of transforming the communities we serve. The church has the answer but must utilize the resources and financial principles available to enhance the gospel message. Too much time is spent doing church work and not the work of the church. Too much time is wasted building personal kingdoms and agendas. It's denial to have all the tools, knowledge, personnel, talents, gifts, and finances in place for the task yet fail to get the job done and then make excuses why it was not done.

Why, you say, has failure been the pattern? It is quite simple. Just look around you, or better yet, look right where you are. With no strings attached giving and hundreds of millions of dollars available for real mission and ministry, who has made you aware of such resources? On the other hand, who has said to you that we will not participate in faith-based funding initiatives? Have you noticed that money is in abundance? Have you noticed the squandering of that abundance? Have you noticed a strain on churches as their resources continue to fluctuate? Why is it that most churches that have families with children do not have after-school care and tutorials? Why is it that many districts with ten to twenty churches do not invest in or manage senior citizen centers or nursing facilities? Every church within a community of 2,000 or more should have community outreach initiatives. Every church should have strategies of demographic growth or relocation and plans for merging or growth.

Suppose there are five churches within a three-to-five-mile radius. Those five churches have annual revenues of $700,000. There are five pastors and no paid education directors, no paid and trained ministers of music, and no paid youth ministers. These five churches have no child development centers and no nursing or assisted living facilities, yet these churches are full of seniors in need of care as well as children who need after-school services and care. What if through a thorough demographic study and plan these five churches utilized funding available to provide such a tremendous and necessary ministry as well as pool the financial resources for relevant ministries within that three-to-five-mile community? What would the possibilities look like? What if the gifts and administrative talents of each pastor were joined under one umbrella, each serving as paid staff in the ministry gift they possess? What would the possibilities look like? The church that persistently and definitively plans and implements ministries that meet the needs of the community she serves will be the church that experiences growth and development.

It is time for the church to take control of and display the power of the gospel she says she possesses. There are too many resources, too much revenue, and too many gifted people not to experience victory and development in every area of our communities. Jesus was and is concerned about the total person and how we live here as well as where we will spend eternity. The beneficiaries of his sacrificial death, burial, and resurrection should do more to bring into fruition the salvific benefit he died to bring his people into. It is just a matter of finalizing plans to make it happen. As a pastor who has laid the foundational work to see such endeavors take place, I can wholeheartedly say it can happen and it must happen. After all, people's souls are at stake, and that is the most important development Jesus desires for his people, which will eventually lead to the development of the other important areas of their life.

I do pray and hope that conviction, inspection, and investigation become the order of the day. It is my prayer that the spirit in which this work was written will be received.

The final chapter of this work will deal with some propositions that I feel must be declared in order to truly experience the fullness of God's purpose and intent for the wholeness of his people on Earth. To you, O Lord, be glory, honor, majesty, and praise!

PART IV
· · · · · · · ·

The Propositions

TEN

Summary and Conclusion

The creation of this work has truly been a provocative challenge as well as a wonderful opportunity. So many people are deserving of much thanks for allowing me the time to complete this book. So many deserve thanks for their critique of this work so that it may be a representative work. I want to take this time to say to you thank you so much for your wonderful spirit of sharing and caring.

As I began this literary journey, I thought it to be an important work that would stir the soul of the complacent and encourage the heart of the progressive. It was to provoke the provocateur to prick the mindsets of the laid-back and satisfied. It was also to convict those in a state of denial pronouncing the clarion cry that all is well when the truth of the matter is all is not well! My intent was to raise issues that would be dramatized in a setting of resolution and resolve for a people needing only to refocus, for their hearts' desire is clear. I have lifted up everything, from my personal vantage point, from a new life in Christ to the enticing of that life to become corrupt in some way. I have tried to accentuate those ills and isms that pollute the very fiber of our confession and profession, creating within leadership a more relevant, progressive, and aggressive radicalism that's so needed for the kingdom in a time like this.

Hence, our first proposition is: trample underfoot the passive tendency of allowing tradition to order the footsteps of our future. Our dictate should be the mission mandates of our Lord, Jesus Christ. The vision of leadership necessary to enhance the fruition of those mission mandates should not be to simply maintain a tradition, but to cause the conviction of that tradition to create relevant strategies to enhance every local church's opportunity to carry out the mission! Every leader should be concerned with the business of networking businesses, banks, bounty holders, and the Bible, leveraging the resources needed for the local church to do mission and ministry without any kind of interference, competition, or usurping. Since the local church is the bread and butter of all other existing departments or organizations, it stands to reason that it is the entity that deserves the development resources to continue the work of Christ on Earth.

People and positions are generated in all other phases of the body through the local church. Their training, loyalty, nurturing, and spiritual walk began at the local church. When the local church is not equipped to provide what the congregation supporting her needs, a stalemate is formed. Loyalty and support to the church will be enhanced, enjoyed, and increased when that local church can see that leadership is concerned about the same by providing presence and provision through not taking away but giving back. The leadership should facilitate the unified effort of all the churches under that authority to network with a certain bank, agency or business or create its own. Leadership should facilitate the leverage now held in abeyance to promote ministry and mission within their control. Leadership should facilitate efforts other than "monuments to men" and perhaps enhance the same through senior citizen housing and counseling centers (for both laypersons and clergy without repercussion). Leadership should facilitate grants and other funding initiatives for every local church to provide ministries germane to the congregation and community. Just a thought!

I asked one leader of a great church, who now sits at the throne of God, why church conglomerates wouldn't build their own hotel and convention center facilities. To my dismay and disappointment, the answer was, "what will we do with it when we are not using it?" I immediately shut down that conversation. I accepted the fact that this was another way of saying that with all the responsibility placed on our leaders they simply could not manage and maintain anything else. We will set forth a preamble that will shut down passivism and promote radical and relevant models of ministry.

We set forth these propositions as an introduction to the positive action that will take place within the body of Christ because of this work. I set forth a preamble that the focus of development and ministry will be the local church and pastor rather than a paradigm where other entities compete with that dynamic and don't enhance it. Leaders other than the pastor should stay out of the church other than to support the ministry and pastor.

That brings me to my second suggestive proposition: leadership will promote a comradeship between clergy of all ranks instead of constant egotistical confrontations between them. If two leaders in an organization are divided in their leadership roles, how can the organization stand or move forward? We must revive the leadership model that promotes with merit due to the kingdom service they have rendered. This should be the substitute and standard rather than misplaced favoritism, vendettas, and political maneuvering. Dirt slinging and wickedness in the church is not of God but straight from the pits of HELL! Either we embrace it and die or destroy it and live.

My third proposition is one of integrity in finances. All churches will set forth a preamble that each entity in the church has quarterly certified audits by a reputable external accounting firm, with that entity reporting on IRS Form 941. The lack of integrity within the framework of a proper stewardship model is destructive. There has been too much "private inurement" practiced by leadership without discipline. It stands to reason that if an organization cannot undergo scrutiny then suspicion is in order. Only financial impropriety hides from and behind "I did not know." What is lost in the process is what kind of posterity we are creating by looking the other way when we know what is really happening. Also lost in the process is the integrity and character of the church because of a few uncaring and unconcerned. I believe the key element to turning the prosperity of the church around is to promote and set forth a preamble that financial integrity and reporting will be of primary concern, and it can be done without strangling the opportunity for leaders to be rightly compensated.

My fourth suggestive proposition is that the church will set forth policies that all pastors be required to hold a master's degree, or at least a bachelor's degree, in a field of religion, divinity, or theology. Further, these would-be pastors would apprentice with an experienced pastor for a minimum of one year prior to accepting a charge. The church will also set forth policies that lay leaders be trained in the field of ministry administration to which they are called, nominated, and elected to serve. With this proposition we will ensure that training and development of all lay leaders in an organized school of learning within their local area for at least a six-month period is of primary interest. Seminars, workshops, yearly creedal analysis, and Saturday morning assemblies are not enough. The church will set forth a preamble that people are taught basic foundational principles until they are able to demonstrate an understanding of them and apply them in their daily walk and office. The day of electing a person to office because he or she had a good campaign speech or enough money to buy votes, or his or her mama served there, should be trampled underfoot. If we are to attract people to the church, the church must offer qualified and trained personnel and ministries to serve the needs of those who come. Leaders cannot lead people where they have not been or are not going.

Finally, the church will set forth a proposition to implement tools, plans, resolutions, and policies that are already in place designed to enhance the growth and development of the church, temporally and spiritually. Failure to implement those policies should have the same repercussions as those that any top-tier manager faces. Why should people of grace operate under a lesser standard than the world? If current leadership and managerial models do not possess the abilities to implement the above process, then let careful perusal of the church and the corporate structure begin to find individuals who can. What is of most importance is the survival and progress of the church, not personal egos and agendas.

The church, in the world, is at a "critical mass" stage. Radical and progressive change is necessary—not wished for or hoped for, but necessary! Those leaving the ranks of the church are not just misfits, nonconformists, or antagonists. Many of them want to see progressive and practical faith models set in place requisite to the needs of a different paradigm, but rather than be part of something not right, they will just leave. When leadership and followership hold onto that, which only relics a memory, people find a way out to practice a different faith model.

Subsequently, however, in all of this maze and mayhem of church stuff, there must be an assessment and analysis of current trends to see if they not only enhance the present church, but secure the future church. For if the current trend of unfair and incomplete disclosure and intentional attacks on pastors and laity holds true to form, we are in serious trouble. For as I peruse the horizon of the church, I see a trend of unholiness, an unethical disregard for leaders, and a divide within the ranks of the laity that exemplifies darkness.

A spirit is invading the very fiber of the church that "attacks and destroys" rather than "attracts and develops." No one wants to remain where they are not wanted, needed, appreciated, developed, or productive.

As I conclude this work, I am reminded of Matthew 24:12, (because iniquity shall abound, the love of many shall wax cold). Perhaps that is the spirit we are dealing with at present. In the meantime, our ability to "bring in the sheaves," create an effective evangelism, and keep those who come to the church continues to diminish. You say this is a prophecy of doom and gloom; well, not according to the last two evangelistic quadrennial reports from mainline denominations. According to that report 53,000 people a week are leaving the mainline denominations. To me that is a cause for alarm and change. This should be the hour of elevated standard, integrity, and character, not a specialized denial of existing conditions. Current conditions also usher in the need for careful analysis of the current trends in mainline denominations to see if in fact they are positioned to compete with other evangelistic models, meet the needs of congregants and would-be congregants, and solidify the posterity of the church. Oh, I know, God will provide, and he does, thank goodness, but I am also cognizant of the fact that God uses human beings to do his will in the earthly realm.

People care about the church. They simply do not care for stagnation, and they look to leadership to provide the marching orders out of this chaos.

After years of pastoral experience, corporate level management, political and civic involvement, financial planning, taxation and asset management, and nonprofit academics, I believe the church is on the verge of a major Pentecost or Armageddon. What is certain is that the decision is up to those leading the church. Everything does rise or fall on leadership. Also certain, is that there is a movement to establish the will of God in the Earth realm that is stronger than the spirit of destruction of this institution, within and without. Psalms 92:13 (Those that be planted in the house of the Lord shall flourish in the courts of our God) gives perpetual hope that the framers of this movement to establish God's will in the Earth realm must be committed and convinced that they will make God's house a house of prayer rather than a den of thieves.

ABOUT THE AUTHOR

The Reverend William L. Neill is a twenty-two-year veteran pastor of the African Methodist Episcopal Zion Church. Pastor Neill has served in a number of leadership positions within the connectional, episcopal, conference, and district church and the community. He has served as either president or a leading officer of the Ministerial Alliance within each geographical area he has pastored. He holds a Bachelor of Science degree and a Master of Arts in Religion  from Liberty University. He is a graduate of the North Carolina Rural Economic Development Center Institute. He is a former candidate for the North Carolina Senate, Fifth District. He is a former member of the Halifax, Edgecombe, Wilson Counties Enterprise Alliance of North Carolina, a Clinton-Gore grassroots initiative for Enterprise Communities and Empowerment Zones across the United States. Neill is also a former regional vice president of the A.L. Williams sales and marketing firm (now Primerica Financial Services Marketing Corporation, a Citigroup affiliate) where he held an insurance license and a Series 6 and 63 registration with the National Association of Securities Dealers. Pastor Neill has won numerous awards and recognition for leadership excellence and service, including Who's Who among Young African-American Leaders. An excellent teacher and preacher and an accomplished vocalist, Neill brings a wealth of knowledge and talent to the living church.

Pastor Neill is the founder of the St. John Community Development Corporation in Wilson, North Carolina, established when he was the pastor of the church. He also serves as a member of the North Carolina Council of Churches Nominating Comittee and a former member of the Councils Economic Justice Committee. He worked close with Barbara (Earls) Zelter, a former leader of economic justice with the council, on special projects like the "Jubilee" project, an initiative that promoted "welware to work" initiatives.

Contact information:

Reverend William L. Neill
 P.O. Box 1785
Fayetteville, NC 28302
(252) 230-4333
 Email: neil54@embarqmail.com

Breinigsville, PA USA
22 September 2009
224491BV00001B/6/P

9 781604 940800